RECONSTRUCTION

Other books in the
Opposing Viewpoints in World History series:

The Cold War
The French Revolution
Immigration
Slavery

RECONSTRUCTION

Laura K. Egendorf, *Book Editor*

Daniel Leone, *President*
Bonnie Szumski, *Publisher*
Scott Barbour, *Managing Editor*
Helen Cothran, *Senior Editor*

OPPOSING
VIEWPOINTS®
SERIES

GREENHAVEN
PRESS®

THOMSON
—————★—————™
GALE

San Diego • Detroit • New York • San Francisco • Cleveland
New Haven, Conn. • Waterville, Maine • London • Munich

THOMSON
✴ ™
GALE

© 2004 by Greenhaven Press. Greenhaven Press is an imprint of The Gale Group, Inc., a division of Thomson Learning, Inc.

Greenhaven® and Thomson Learning™ are trademarks used herein under license.

For more information, contact
Greenhaven Press
27500 Drake Rd.
Farmington Hills, MI 48331-3535
Or you can visit our Internet site at http://www.gale.com

Cover credit: © Medford Historical Society Collection/CORBIS
Dover Publications, 60
Library of Congress, 85, 102, 119, 147

LIBRARY OF CONGRESS CATALOGING-IN-PUBLICATION DATA

Reconstruction : opposing viewpoints in world history / Laura K. Egendorf, book editor.
    p. cm. — (Opposing viewpoints in world history series)
    Includes bibliographical references and index.
    ISBN 0-7377-1704-1 (pbk. : alk. paper) — ISBN 0-7377-1703-3 (lib. : alk. paper)
    1. Reconstruction. 2. Reconstruction—Sources. I. Egendorf, Laura K., 1973– . II. Series.
    E668.R4155 2004
    973.8—dc21
                                                 2003049016

Printed in the United States of America

Contents

are biologically and culturally different from white Americans.

Chapter 4: Historians Debate Reconstruction

 **Foreword**

On December 2, 1859, several hundred soldiers gathered at the outskirts of Charles Town, Virginia, to carry out, and provide security for, the execution of a shabbily dressed old man with a beard that hung to his chest. The execution of John Brown quickly became and has remained one of those pivotal historical events that are immersed in controversy. Some of Brown's contemporaries claimed that he was a religious fanatic who deserved to be executed for murder. Others claimed Brown was a heroic and selfless martyr whose execution was a tragedy. Historians have continued to debate which picture of Brown is closest to the truth.

The wildly diverging opinions on Brown arise from fundamental disputes involving slavery and race. In 1859 the United States was becoming increasingly polarized over the issue of slavery. Brown believed in both the necessity of violence to end slavery and in the full political and social equality of the races. This made him part of the radical fringe even in the North. Brown's conviction and execution stemmed from his role in leading twenty-one white and black followers to attack and occupy a federal weapons arsenal in Harpers Ferry, Virginia. Brown had hoped to ignite a large slave uprising. However, the raid begun on October 16, 1859, failed to draw support from local slaves; after less than thirty-six hours, Brown's forces were overrun by federal and local troops. Brown was wounded and captured, and ten of his followers were killed.

Brown's raid—and its intent to arm slaves and foment insurrection—was shocking to the South and much of the North. An editorial in the *Patriot*, an Albany, Georgia, newspaper, stated that Brown was a "notorious old thief and murderer" who deserved to be hanged. Many southerners expressed fears that Brown's actions were part of a broader northern conspiracy against the South—fears that seemed to be confirmed by captured letters documenting Brown's ties with some prominent northern abolitionists, some of whom had provided him with financial support. Such alarms also found confirmation in the pronouncements of some speakers such as writer Henry David Thoreau, who asserted that

Brown had "a perfect right to interfere by force with the slave-holder, in order to rescue the slave." But not all in the North defended Brown's actions. Abraham Lincoln and William Seward, leading politicians of the nascent Republican Party, both denounced Brown's raid. Abolitionists, including William Lloyd Garrison, called Brown's adventure "misguided, wild, and apparently insane." They were afraid Brown had done serious damage to the abolitionist cause.

Today, though all agree that Brown's ideas on racial equality are no longer radical, historical opinion remains divided on just what Brown thought he could accomplish with his raid, or even whether he was fully sane. Historian Russell Banks argues that even today opinions of Brown tend to split along racial lines. African Americans tend to view him as a hero, Banks argues, while whites are more likely to judge him mad. "And it's for the same reason—because he was a white man who was willing to sacrifice his life to liberate Black Americans. The very thing that makes him seem mad to white Americans is what makes him seem heroic to Black Americans."

The controversy over John Brown's life and death remind readers that history is replete with debate and controversy. Not only have major historical developments frequently been marked by fierce debates as they happened, but historians examining the same events in retrospect have often come to opposite conclusions about their causes, effects, and significance. By featuring both contemporaneous and retrospective disputes over historical events in a pro/con format, the Opposing Viewpoints in World History series can help readers gain a deeper understanding of important historical issues, see how historical judgments unfold, and develop critical thinking skills. Each article is preceded by a concise summary of its main ideas and information about the author. An in-depth book introduction and prefaces to each chapter provide background and context. An annotated table of contents and index help readers quickly locate material of interest. Each book also features an extensive bibliography for further research, questions designed to spark discussion and promote close reading and critical thinking, and a chronology of events.

 Introduction

> "Studying works on Reconstruction . . . can provide a fairly clear notion of the problems confronting the periods in which historians lived but not always as clear a picture of Reconstruction itself."
>
> —John Hope Franklin

In a speech delivered in front of the American Historical Association in 1979, association president and Howard University history professor John Hope Franklin declared, "It may be said that every generation since 1870 has written the history of the Reconstruction era. And what historians have written tells as much about their own generation as about the Reconstruction period itself." Franklin was speaking from experience; his 1961 landmark work *Reconstruction: After the Civil War*, which has helped shape interpretations of Reconstruction for more than four decades, was informed by the civil rights movement that developed after World War II. In Franklin's time black Americans were seeking to regain some of the political and social equality they had enjoyed briefly during the first years of Reconstruction, when the nation passed several civil rights bills and amendments granting black men the right to vote and prohibiting certain kinds of racial discrimination.

Franklin's work also served to counter what had been the dominant critique of Reconstruction, William Archibald Dunning's late nineteenth-century theory that the failure of Reconstruction could be blamed on carpetbaggers (northern Republicans who migrated to the South after the Civil War), scalawags (southern Republicans who had remained loyal to the Union), and freed slaves. Franklin, in contrast, defended the actions of southern blacks and their white supporters and blamed the era's failings on President Andrew Johnson and conservative white southerners. The differing views held by these two men is likely due to the eras in which they lived. Dunning lived and wrote during a time when corruption in Republican governments was a recurring problem, which may explain his distaste for the Republican Party, while

Franklin's work was published as the post–World War II civil rights movement was reaching its peak. The opposing interpretations of Dunning and Franklin show that as society has changed over time, people's understanding of Reconstruction has also changed. Because historical interpretation is always colored by the era in which the historian lives, a definitive interpretation of major events such as Reconstruction will likely never be reached.

Although Reconstruction is generally understood to have spanned from 1865, when the Civil War ended, to 1877, when the remaining federal troops were withdrawn from the South, plans to reunite the United States and rebuild the South began as early as 1863. With the Union army in control of large swaths of the Confederacy by late 1863, President Abraham Lincoln began to develop a plan for reconstruction that included amnesty and pardons for inhabitants of the rebellious states. However, Lincoln's assassination precluded the institution of his plan. The responsibility for Reconstruction fell to his successor, Andrew Johnson, who found himself at odds with Radical Republicans—men such as Pennsylvania congressman Thaddeus Stevens whose primary goals were to provide freed slaves with civil rights and prevent southern white Democrats from controlling former Confederate governments. The Radical Republicans, who, for the most part, dominated government, achieved some of their goals, most notably the passages of the Civil Rights Acts of 1866 and 1875 (although much of the latter was overturned by the Supreme Court in 1883) and the ratification of the Thirteenth, Fourteenth, and Fifteenth Amendments to the U.S. Constitution, which ended slavery, made blacks citizens, and gave them the right to vote, respectively. However, the president and moderate and conservative forces in the House and Senate were able to thwart many Radical goals. The Radical Republicans' power began to fade in the late 1860s and early 1870s, and by the 1876 presidential election, they had little power in the South. It was during the first two decades following the Radical Republicans' weakened position in the South that William Archibald Dunning began his influential scholarship.

Born in New Jersey in 1857, William Archibald Dunning's interest in Reconstruction was initially sparked by his father. The younger Dunning continued his explorations while a student at

Columbia University, the school where he would later become a political science professor. At the age of twenty-eight, he published *The Constitution of the United States in Civil War and Reconstruction, 1860–1867.* In his introduction to an edition of Dunning's 1898 collection, *Essays on the Civil War and Reconstruction*, David Donald explains that Dunning's 1885 tome had three key effects: It made post–Civil War history a respectable field for scholars; it secured Dunning's employment at Columbia, where he would work for the rest of his life; and "it caused Dunning to be sought out by some of the very best graduate students entering the field of history." His influence, however, went beyond Columbia— Dunning was president of both the American Historical Association and the American Political Science Association.

In addition to his 1885 and 1898 works, Dunning penned *Reconstruction, Political and Economic: 1865–1877*, published in 1907. His books centered on the theory that, as explained by University of Arkansas professor Carl H. Moneyhon, "the Republicans represented the worst elements of society: ignorant blacks, malicious southern whites, and 'carpetbaggers.'" Dunning believed that Reconstruction failed because of the incompetency and corruption of the Radical Republican state governments that were established in the South in the mid-to-late 1860s. In *Reconstruction, Political and Economic*, Dunning questioned the administrative and economic skills of "the ambitious northern whites, inexperienced southern whites, and unintelligent blacks who controlled the first reconstructed governments." He was especially critical of their financial decisions, asserting that these new governments worsened state debts by increasing spending on new jobs and salaries. Dunning's questioning of the Reconstruction Republicans was shaped, as Donald explains, by the corruption of Republican governments in the 1870s and 1880s. During that era in American history— known derisively as the "Gilded Age," after a novel by Mark Twain and Charles Dudley Warner—Republican politicians, including members of the Grant administration, often became entangled in suspicious dealings with oil and railroad barons or traded lucrative civil-service jobs for votes.

Incompetency and corruption were not Dunning's only targets. He also wrote extensively on the new rights granted to blacks and the efforts of southern governments to limit those freedoms. In *Reconstruction, Political and Economic*, Dunning asserted that black suffrage embittered southern white Democrats—many of whom were plantation owners—who failed to convince the newly franchised blacks to vote with their former masters. Dunning sided with the Democrats, expressing his concern for what he considered the lack of political understanding by blacks: "Without a clear comprehension as to what it all meant, the mass of the freedmen were sure that they must be Union men and Republicans." In addition, as Donald explains, Dunning believed that the causes of the South's trouble were rooted in efforts to force the black and white races to coexist. Donald writes, "Slavery, [Dunning] declared, had provided 'a *modus vivendi* through which social life was possible,' and any subsequent political arrangement in the South, to be enduring, must recognize 'the same fact of racial inequality.'" Dunning's support for southern white Democrats was also indicated by his defense of black codes, laws passed by southern legislatures that placed a number of restrictions on blacks, including prohibitions on jury service, intermarriage, and leases. Northerners believed that southern governments used these codes as a way to subjugate blacks and make them nearly as powerless as they had been before emancipation. Dunning disagreed, writing that the purpose of these laws was "to bring some sort of order out of the social and economic chaos which a full acceptance of the results of war and emancipation involved. . . . The freedmen were not, and in the nature of the case could not for generations be, on the same social, moral, and intellectual plane with the whites; and this fact was recognized by constituting them a separate class in the social order." Dunning opined that the "well-established traits and habits of the negroes" justified restrictions on some civil rights such as gun ownership and the right of blacks to testify in court.

The Freedmen's Bureau was another target of Dunning's opprobrium. Established by Congress in March 1865, the bureau was intended to aid newly freed slaves and southern white refugees. Although the bureau was successful in some respects, for example establishing more than four thousand schools, its fate was determined by the antipathy of President Johnson and most white southerners. Dunning wrote of the bureau agents:

> However much tact and practical good sense the local agent
> was able to bring to the performance of his delicate duties, he
> in most cases, being a northern man, was wholly unable to
> take a view of the situation that could make him agreeable to
> the whites of the neighborhood. He saw in both freedman and
> former master qualities which the latter could never admit.
> Hence the working of the bureau, with its intrusion into the
> fundamental relationships of social life, engendered violent
> hostility from the outset on the part of the whites.

The Freedmen's Bureau dissolved in 1872. Five years later, Reconstruction ended as well. Under the Compromise of 1877, Democrats agreed to give Republican presidential candidate Rutherford
B. Hayes twenty disputed electoral votes, thereby awarding him the
presidency, in exchange for the withdrawal of federal troops from
the South and the end of federal interference in southern state governments. For Dunning the compromise was an appropriate and
necessary conclusion to Reconstruction. He declared:

> Generalized, this famous bargain meant: Let the reforming
> Republicans direct the national government and the south-
> ern whites may rule the negroes. Such were the terms on
> which the [Hayes] administration took up its task. They pre-
> cisely and consciously reversed the principles of reconstruc-
> tion as followed under [President Ulysses S.] Grant, and
> hence they ended an era. Grant in 1868 had cried peace, but
> in his time, with the radicals and carpet-baggers in the sad-
> dle, there was no peace; with Hayes peace came.

However, Dunning was not completely critical of Republicans.
He praised Reconstruction governments for establishing a system
of universal public education in the South and acknowledged that
while many government officials were corrupt and incompetent,
the higher-ups in the Freedmen's Bureau and state governments
were honest and showed good judgment. In the end, however, as
University of Maryland professor Herman Belz explains, "In Dunning's view, the purpose of Reconstruction was to give freedmen
and white Unionists power to organize governments and control

the former Confederate states indefinitely."

Dunning's impact was far-reaching. As a professor Dunning mentored a number of students, men and women who would become known collectively as the Dunning school. The most notable of these students were southerners, among them Walter L. Fleming, who wrote *The Civil War and Reconstruction in Alabama*, and W.W. Davis, author of *The Civil War and Reconstruction, in Florida*. Donald writes of these students, "[Their] dissertations . . . provide our basic knowledge of the political history of the South during the postwar years. Yet, with every conscious desire to be fair, these students of Dunning shaped their monographs to accord with the white Southerners' view that the Negro was innately inferior." Dunning's students condoned the Ku Klux Klan and other white terrorist organizations while decrying blacks' involvement in Reconstruction governments. However, these racist beliefs cannot be considered to completely mirror Dunning's beliefs. Donald contends, "Dunning allowed his students to pursue their own paths, and it is hardly surprising that his young Southerners, themselves products of the dark days that followed Reconstruction, should have adopted sharply sectional views." Roberta Sue Alexander, who teaches history at the University of Dayton, suggests that the racism and nationalism that marked the United States at the turn of the twentieth century influenced the Dunning school.

Responding to Dunning

Although there were a few exceptions, such as civil rights leader W.E.B. Du Bois's 1910 article "Reconstruction and Its Benefits" and 1935 book *Black Reconstruction*, the Dunning school of thought went largely unquestioned until the 1960s. In his article "The New View of Reconstruction," historian Eric Foner explains, "Anyone who attended high school before 1960 learned that Reconstruction was an era of unrelieved sordidness in American political and social life."

By 1960, however, the American political climate was changing. In November the nation voted the liberal John Fitzgerald Kennedy into the White House. Meanwhile, a civil rights movement had been in full swing since the mid-1950s. With black Americans once again engaged in a struggle to achieve political and social equality, the time was ripe for a new look at Reconstruction. The leader of this new school was John Hope Franklin.

Franklin joined the history department at historically black Howard University in 1947. One year later, according to Professor Alexander, Franklin "called for a new direction in Reconstruction historiography, one rejecting interpretations that, like those of William Dunning, treated blacks with contempt, ignored Presidential Reconstruction, and saw southern whites uncritically as heroes." The synthesis of Franklin's ideas culminated in the 1961 publication of his book *Reconstruction: After the Civil War*, labeled by Alexander "the first major synthesis of the revisionist interpretation of Reconstruction."

Franklin's perspective on Reconstruction was almost point-for-point the exact opposite of Dunning's. While Franklin acknowledged that Radical Republican governments were often corrupt, he mostly defended the actions taken by freed blacks, southern white Republicans, and what he termed "so-called carpetbaggers." Unlike Dunning and his pupils, who questioned the political know-how of blacks, Franklin lauded the skills and aspirations of black politicians such as South Carolina treasurer Francis L. Car-

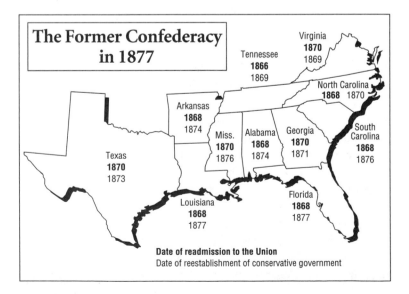

The Former Confederacy in 1877

Virginia
1870
1869

Tennessee
1866
1869

North Carolina
1868 1870

Arkansas
1868
1874

Miss.
1870
1876

Alabama
1868
1874

Georgia
1870
1871

South Carolina
1868
1876

Texas
1870
1873

Louisiana
1868
1877

Florida
1868
1877

Date of readmission to the Union
Date of reestablishment of conservative government

dozo and Mississippi legislator (and future congressman) John Roy Lynch. Franklin further asserted that rather than try to demoralize and dominate white southerners, black politicians were largely conciliatory—for example, they sought to allow ex-Confederates, who in the period immediately following the war had been stripped of many of their civil rights, to again vote and hold office. He also maintained that freedmen had little desire to instigate an economic or social revolution: "Negroes attempted no revolution in the social relations of the races in the South. . . . Negroes, as a rule, conceded to the insistence of whites that they were a race apart; and they made little or no attempt to destroy white supremacy except where such supremacy rejected Negroes altogether as human beings."

Franklin also sought to refurbish the image of carpetbaggers and scalawags. Previous historians, Franklin observed, had described Republicans who migrated from the North as "gangs of itinerant adventurers, vagrant interlopers," men who sought the economic and political exploitation of southerners for their own personal gains. According to Franklin, these purported "carpetbaggers" were more interested in building up industries, especially iron and coal, in the South, than in taking over local and state governments. He writes, "[These] so-called carpetbaggers were not simply Radicals with no consideration for the welfare and development of the South," adding that many of these migrants were well liked by white southerners. Franklin further asserted that white southerners known as "scalawags" had been misjudged. While he acknowledged that they were partially to blame for the graft and corruption that marred Reconstruction governments, "[Their] most serious offense was to have been loyal to the Union during the Civil War or to have declared that they had been loyal and thereby to have enjoyed full citizenship during the period of Radical Reconstruction."

Dunning had treated southern blacks, southern white Republicans, and northern white migrants as a powerful triumvirate, working together to dominate former Confederates. By Franklin's estimation, that coalition was not as united as Dunning had surmised. In fact, according to Franklin, the three groups often found themselves at cross-purposes: "At times the position of the Negro leaders approached that of the crusading abolitionists. Meanwhile, the so-called carpetbaggers frequently preoccupied themselves with building up the alliance between the business community and the Republican-controlled state government. All too often, moreover, the loyal Southerners talked and acted like the conservative former Confederates whom they presumably opposed."

The Freedmen's Bureau and black codes also received different interpretations from Franklin than they had in Dunning's works. Franklin observed that the bureau not only improved education in the South but also protected freedmen's labor rights by enabling them to work at fair wages and choose their employers. Whereas Dunning had castigated bureau agents for interfering in "fundamental relationships" between blacks and whites, Franklin placed the early death of the bureau at the hands of white southerners and President Johnson. He wrote, "It can hardly be said that rule by the former Confederates was by any means destroyed by the Freedmen's Bureau. It would be more accurate to say that the former Confederates, with the aid of President Johnson, did much to destroy the effectiveness of the Bureau." He also contended that the black codes were not a justifiable response to alleged moral and intellectual disparity between the races; rather they exemplified the efforts made by white southerners to maintain supremacy and turn the clock back to the pre–Civil War era. As Franklin explained, "The Confederacy was beaten, but it refused to die. The spirit of the South and the principles underlying it were very much alive. More than that, those who had fought against the Union were in control, pursuing most of their prewar policies as though there had never been a war."

The efforts of southern Democrats known as Redeemers to regain control of their region reached fruition in 1877. While Dunning believed that the Compromise of 1877 brought peace to the United States, Franklin looked upon it as a way for the South to "[retreat] further from democracy and . . . institutionalize and make permanent the redemption policies by which it had overthrown reconstruction." Within a generation southern states had instituted poll taxes and literacy tests that made it nearly impossible for blacks to vote and had also instituted laws that relegated blacks to low-paying and menial jobs.

A Changing Society

Other important new looks at Reconstruction followed in the path of Franklin's *Reconstruction: After the Civil War*. These books included 1965's *The Era of Reconstruction, 1865–1877*, written by Kenneth Stampp; Avery Craven's 1969 book, *Reconstruction: The Ending of the Civil War;* Rembert W. Patrick's *The Reconstruction of the Nation*, published in 1967; and Hans Trefousse's 1971 *Reconstruction: America's First Effort at Racial Democracy*. Although these authors did not agree on every point, they largely followed Franklin's lead, evincing greater sympathy toward freedmen and northern and southern white Republicans. All of these books were written in the wake of the successes of the 1960s civil rights movement, in particular the June 1964 passage of a civil rights bill that outlawed racial discrimination in public places (the first such bill since the ill-fated Civil Rights Act of 1875). As had been the case during the height of Reconstruction, the United States was once again led by a southern president named Johnson; only this time, the president came from Texas, not Tennessee, and Lyndon Baines Johnson encouraged, rather than vetoed, civil rights legislation. With support for civil rights in the United States reaching previously unknown heights, it is not surprising that the radical forces behind Reconstruction were examined in a more favorable light.

Reconstruction is one of the most controversial periods in American history, and it is unlikely that historians will cease interpreting those twelve complex years. However, as American society changes, so too will the nation's attitude toward the efforts made to rebuild the United States after the Civil War. While there will likely never be a definitive interpretation of Reconstruction, the opposing perspectives offered by key Reconstruction figures and prominent historians can provide students and other interested readers with a general understanding of the era. In *Opposing Viewpoints in World History: Reconstruction*, the authors evaluate the highlights and lowlights of Reconstruction in the following chapters: Reconstructing a Nation: Opposing Plans; Conflicts During Reconstruction; The New Social Order; and Historians Debate Reconstruction. In these chapters the contributors show not only how difficult the reunion of the North and South was but also how complex historical interpretation can be.

CHAPTER 1

Reconstructing a Nation: Opposing Plans

# Chapter Preface

The Civil War devastated the South. One out of every three of the soldiers who had enlisted in the Confederate army died, for a total of 260,000 fatalities. Civilians saw the cornerstone of the South—its land and plantations—destroyed by vanquishing northern troops. In the wake of the war, countless southerners suffered not only from the humiliation of losing to the North but also from hunger, a lack of clean water, and homelessness. With the young men who might have been able to rebuild the southern economy dead, and the Emancipation Proclamation ridding the South of its slave-based economy, the region experienced an economic collapse. Land values dropped precipitously at the war's end; property in Virginia that had sold for one hundred dollars per acre before the war was now being offered for two dollars per acre. Thomas A. Bailey and David M. Kennedy explain in *The American Pageant: A History of the Republic, Volume II:* "Agriculture—the economic lifeblood of the South—was almost hopelessly crippled. Once white-cotton fields now yielded a lush harvest of nothing but green weeds."

The dire conditions of the South naturally evoked much sorrow and bitterness in the regions' white inhabitants, which made the task of reconstruction that much harder. Many northerners traveled to the South in order to understand southern attitudes in hopes of aiding reconstruction efforts. Indeed, it seemed reasonable to assume that in order to bring the southern states back into the Union successfully, it was necessary to understand the level of southern resistance to that end and determine what other problems, especially social, might hamper reconstruction efforts. Two northern observers with these goals in mind were Carl Schurz and Benjamin C. Truman. Schurz made a fairly negative assessment of white southerners' attitudes toward their conquerors and the now-freed slaves while Truman offered a more positive view of the South.

The German-born Carl Schurz was a major general in the Union army. At the request of President Andrew Johnson, he traveled throughout the South for seventy-nine days in the summer of 1865 in order to assess conditions and attitudes in the region. Schurz detailed his observations in *Report on the Condition of the South*, published by the Senate later that year. He noted that disorder and violence marked the South, adding that blacks were frequently the victims of assaults and murders. Much of this violence toward former slaves, claimed Schurz, stemmed from the southern belief that blacks would not work unless they were physically compelled to do so.

Schurz was particularly concerned about southerners' attitudes toward northerners and the federal government. He wrote that the Union soldiers stationed in the South were seen as intruders and strangers, adding "[these feelings] of aversion and resentment . . . extend beyond the limits of the army, to the people of the north." However, Schurz believed that this enmity would subside once southerners shed their old attitudes and began to work together with northerners. His greater fear was that southerners were not truly loyal to the United States: "There is, as yet, among the southern people an *utter absence of national feeling.*" In his book *The Reconstruction of the Nation*, Rembert W. Patrick concludes, "Schurz found Southerners unrepentant, worshipping their Confederate heroes, and determined to fix the Negro's status at some intermediate point between slavery and freedom."

Unlike Schurz, newspaper correspondent Benjamin C. Truman, who traveled the South from September 1865 to March 1866, did not believe that white southerners mistreated former slaves. While he acknowledged that poor whites tried to keep blacks out of higher-paid skilled jobs, Truman contended, "It is the former slave-owners who are the best friends the negro has in the south." He added that southern planters had a better understanding of the black work ethic than did the northerners that rented plantations from impoverished southern owners; he also observed that blacks preferred working for southern employers. Contrary to Schurz's contentions, Truman claimed that the northerners who moved to the South were treated with respect. He also asserted that the former rebellious states displayed a growing loyalty toward the federal government: "It is my belief that the south—the great, substantial, and prevailing element—is more loyal now than it was at the end of the war—more loyal to-day than yesterday, and that it will be more loyal tomorrow than to-day."

These conflicting observations on life in the South after the Civil War made the already challenging path to reconstruction even more difficult. The authors in the following chapter evaluate several other controversies that served to complicate reconstruction, including how the federal government should treat the conquered states and whether reconstruction is an executive or legislative responsibility.

Viewpoint 1

"To all persons who have, directly or by implication, participated in the existing rebellion, . . . a full pardon is hereby granted to them."

Reconstruction Is an Executive Function

Abraham Lincoln

By the middle of 1863, after the Union army's successful occupation of Tennessee, Louisiana, and North Carolina, President Abraham Lincoln had begun to develop plans for the reconstruction of the United States. On December 8, 1863, two years before the end of the war, Lincoln issued the following document, the Proclamation of Amnesty. The proclamation set forth the terms for a reconstruction that would be largely under the purview of the executive branch. In addition, America's sixteenth president argued that the rebel southern states were guilty of treason but noted that he had the authority to grant pardons in particular cases. Lincoln's proclamation outraged the Radical Republicans, who resented his use of the executive prerogative and desired a more severe restructuring of the South to ensure equal treatment of blacks and whites. Lincoln was unable to implement the entirety of his reconstruction plan before his assassination on April 14, 1865.

Abraham Lincoln, "Proclamation of Amnesty," *A Compilation of the Messages and Papers of the Presidents, 1789–1897*, vol. 6, edited by James Richardson. Washington, DC, 1896–1899.

Whereas in and by the Constitution of the United States it is provided that the President "shall have power to grant reprieves and pardons for offenses against the United States, except in cases of impeachment"; and

Whereas a rebellion now exists whereby the loyal state governments of several states have for a long time been subverted, and many persons have committed and and are now guilty of treason against the United States; and

Whereas, with reference to said rebellion and treason, laws have been enacted by Congress declaring forfeitures and confiscation of property and liberation of slaves, all upon terms and conditions therein stated, and also declaring that the President was thereby authorized at any time thereafter, by proclamation, to extend to persons who may have participated in the existing rebellion in any state or part thereof pardon and amnesty, with such exceptions and at such times and on such conditions as he may deem expedient for the public welfare; and

Whereas the congressional declaration for limited and conditional pardon accords with well-established judicial exposition of the pardoning power;

Whereas, with reference to said rebellion, the President of the United States has issued several proclamations with provisions in regard to the liberation of slaves; and

Whereas it is now desired by some persons heretofore engaged in said rebellion to resume their allegiance to the United States and to reinaugurate loyal state governments within and for their respective states:

A Full Pardon

Therefore, I, Abraham Lincoln, President of the United States do proclaim, declare, and make known to all persons who have, directly or by implication, participated in the existing rebellion, except as hereinafter excepted, that a full pardon is hereby granted to them and each of them, with restoration of all rights of property, except as to slaves and in property cases where rights of third parties shall have intervened, and upon the condition that every such person shall take and subscribe an oath and thenceforward keep and maintain said oath inviolate, and which oath shall be

Lincoln's Hopes for the South

In January 1901, Atlantic Monthly *published an issue on Reconstruction. One of the contributors to the issue was Woodrow Wilson, who was then a professor at Princeton University. In the following excerpt from his article, "The Reconstruction of the Southern States," Wilson argues that President Lincoln sought to reunite the South with the rest of the United States without degrading the conquered region.*

It was, in [Lincoln's] view, not the southern states which had taken up arms against the Union, but merely the people dwelling within them. State lines defined the territory within which rebellion had spread and men had organized under arms to destroy the Union; but their organization had been effected without color of law; that could not be a state, in any legal meaning of the term, which denied what was the indispensable prerequisite of its every exercise of political functions, its membership in the Union. He was not fighting states, therefore, or a confederacy of states, but only a body of people who refused to act as states, and could not, if they would, form another Union. What he wished and strove for, without passion save for the accomplishment of his purpose, without enmity against persons, and yet with burning hostility against what the southerners meant to do, was to bring the people of the southern states once more to submission and allegiance; to assist them, when subdued, to rehabilitate the states whose territory and resources, whose very organization, they had used to effect a revolution; to do whatever the circumstances and his own powers, whether as President or merely as an influential man and earnest friend of peace, might render possible to put them back, defeated, but not conquered or degraded, into the old-time hierarchy of the Union.

Woodrow Wilson, *Atlantic Monthly*, January 1901.

registered for permanent preservation and shall be of the tenor and effect following, to wit:

> I,— — —, do solemnly swear, in presence of Almighty God, that I will henceforth faithfully support, protect, and defend the Constitution of the United States and the Union of the states thereunder; and that I will in like manner abide by and faithfully support all acts of Congress passed during the existing rebellion with reference to slaves, so long and so far as not repealed, modified, or held void by Congress or by decision of the Supreme Court; and that I will in like manner abide by and faithfully support all proclamations of the President made during the existing rebellion having reference to slaves, so long and so far as not modified or declared void by decision of the Supreme Court. So help me God.

The persons excepted from the benefits of the foregoing provisions are all who are or shall have been civil or diplomatic officers or agents of the so-called Confederate government; all who have left judicial stations under the United States to aid the rebellion; all who are or shall have been military or naval officers of said so-called Confederate government above the rank of colonel in the Army or of lieutenant in the Navy; all who left seats in the United States Congress to aid the rebellion; all who resigned commissions in the Army or Navy of the United States and afterward aided the rebellion; and all who have engaged in any way in treating colored persons, or white persons in charge of such, otherwise than lawfully as prisoners of war, and which persons may have been found in the United States service as soldiers, seamen, or in any other capacity.

Reestablishing State Governments

And I do further proclaim, declare, and make known that whenever, in any of the states of Arkansas, Texas, Louisiana, Mississippi, Tennessee, Alabama, Georgia, Florida, South Carolina, and North Carolina, a number of persons, not less than one-tenth in number of the votes cast in such state at the presidential election of the year A.D. 1860, each having taken oath aforesaid, and not having since violated it, and being a qualified voter by the election law of the state existing immediately before the so-called act of secession, and excluding all others, shall reestablish a state government which shall be republican and in nowise contravening said oath, such shall be recognized as the true government of the state, and the state shall receive thereunder the benefits of the constitutional provision which declares that "the United States shall guarantee to every state in this Union a republican form of government and shall protect each of them against invasion, and, on application of the legislature, or the executive (when the legislature cannot be convened), against domestic violence."

And I do further proclaim, declare, and make known that any provision which may be adopted by such state government in relation to the freed people of such state which shall recognize and declare their permanent freedom, provide for their education, and which may yet be consistent as a temporary arrangement with their present condition as a laboring, landless, and homeless class will not be objected to by the national executive.

And it is suggested as not improper that in constructing a loyal state government in any state the name of the state, the boundary, the subdivisions, the constitution, and the general code of laws as before the rebellion be maintained, subject only to the modifications made necessary by the conditions hereinbefore stated, and such others, if any, not contravening said conditions and which may be deemed expedient by those framing the new state government.

To avoid misunderstanding, it may be proper to say that this proclamation, so far as it relates to state governments, has no reference to states wherein loyal state governments have all the while been maintained. And for the same reason it may be proper to further say that whether members sent to Congress from any state shall be admitted to seats constitutionally rests exclusively with the respective houses and not to any extent with the executive. And, still further, that this proclamation is intended to present the people of the states wherein the national authority has been suspended and loyal state governments have been subverted a mode in and by which the national authority and loyal state governments may be reestablished within said states or in any of them; and while the mode presented is the best the executive can suggest, with his present impressions, it must not be understood that no other possible mode would be acceptable.

Viewpoint 2

"A more studied outrage on the legislative authority of the people has never been perpetrated."

Reconstruction Is a Legislative Function

Henry Winter Davis

In 1863 Abraham Lincoln proclaimed that the executive branch should be in charge of reconstruction policy, in particular the readmission of rebel states to the Union. His declaration rankled many legislators, in particular Representative Henry Winter Davis and Senator Benjamin Wade. The two congressmen drafted the Wade-Davis bill in response to the president's proposal. The bill, which Congress approved in 1864, gave the legislative branch greater authority over reconstruction and established stricter standards for readmission. However, Lincoln vetoed the bill because he was unwilling to commit to any particular reconstruction plan. Moreover, he felt that states that were already "reconstructed" under his policies would not be able to meet Congress's more rigorous conditions. In the following document, written in the wake of Lincoln's veto and published in the *New York Daily Tribune*, Davis contends that Lincoln has overstepped his executive powers and that Congress is the sole authority in matters of reconstruction.

Henry Winter Davis, "The Wade-Davis Manifesto," *The New York Daily Tribune*, August 5, 1864.

T o the Supporters of the Government:
       We have read without surprise, but not without indigna-
tion the proclamation of the President of the 8th of July, 1864. The
supporters of the administration are responsible to the country
for its conduct, and it is their right and duty to check the en-
croachments of the executive on the authority of Congress, and
to require it to confine itself to its proper sphere. . . .

A Proclamation, Not a Law

The President did not sign the bill to "guarantee to certain States,
whose governments have been usurped, a Republican form of government," passed by the supporters of his Administration in both
houses of Congress, after mature deliberation. The bill did not
therefore become a law, and it is therefore nothing. The proclamation is neither an approval nor a veto of the bill; it is therefore
a document unknown to the laws and Constitution of the United
States. So far as it contains an apology for not signing the bill, it is
a political manifesto against the friends of the government. So far
as it proposes to execute the bill, which is not a law, it is a grave executive usurpation. . . .

Had the proclamation stopped there, it would have been only
one other defeat of the will of the people by an executive perversion of the Constitution. But it goes farther. The President says:

> And whereas the said bill contains, among other things, a plan
> for restoring the States in rebellion to their proper practical
> relations in the Union, which plan expresses the sense of Con-
> gress upon that subject, and which plan it is now thought fit
> to lay before the people for their consideration—

By what authority of the Constitution? In what forms? The result to be declared by whom? With what effect when ascertained?
Is it to be a law by the approval of the people, without the approval
of Congress, at the will of the President? Will the President, on his
opinion of the popular approval, execute it as law? Or is this merely
a device to avoid the serious responsibility of defeating a law on
which so many loyal hearts reposed for security? But the reasons
now assigned for not approving the bill are full of ominous significance. The President proceeds:

Now, therefore, I, Abraham Lincoln, President of the United States do proclaim, declare, and make known that, while I am (as I was in December last when by proclamation I propounded a plan for restoration) unprepared, by a formal approval of this bill, to be inflexibly committed to any single plan of restoration—

That is to say, the President is resolved that the people shall not, by law, take any securities from the rebel States against a renewal of the rebellion, before restoring their power to govern us. His wisdom and prudence are to be our sufficient guarantees! He farther says:

And while I am also unprepared to declare that the Free-state constitutions and governments already adopted and installed in Arkansas and Louisiana shall be set aside and held for naught, thereby repelling and discouraging the loyal citizens who have set up the same as to farther effort—

That is to say, the President persists in recognizing those shadows of governments in Arkansas and Louisiana which Congress formally declared should not be recognized; whose representatives and senators were repelled by formal votes of both houses of Congress, and which, it was formally declared, should have no electoral vote for President and Vice-President. They are mere creatures of his will. They can not live a day without his support. They are mere oligarchies imposed on the people by military orders, under the forms of elections, at which generals, provost-marshals, soldiers, and camp followers were the chief actors, assisted by a handful of resident citizens, and urged on to premature action by private letters from the President. In neither Louisiana nor Arkansas, before [General Nathaniel P.] Banks's defeat, did the United States control half the territory or half the population. In Louisiana, General Banks's proclamation candidly declared, "*The fundamental law of the State is martial law.*" On that foundation of freedom he erected what the President calls "the free Constitution and government of Louisiana. . . ."

The President, by preventing this bill from becoming a law, holds the electoral votes of the rebel States at the dictation of his personal ambition. If these votes turn the balance in his favor, is it to be supposed that his competitor, defeated by such means will acquiesce? If the rebel majority assert their supremacy in those States, and send votes which elect an enemy of the government, will we not repel his claims? And is not that civil war for the presidency inaugurated by the voice of rebel States? Seriously impressed with these dangers, Congress, "the proper constitutional authority," formally declared that there are no governments in the rebel States, and provided for their erection at a proper time. . . . The President's proclamation "holds for naught" this judgment, and discards the authority of the Supreme Court, and strides headlong toward the anarchy his proclamation of the 8th of December inaugurated. If electors for President be allowed to be chosen in either of those States, a sinister light will be cast on the motives which induced the President to "hold for naught" the will of Congress rather than his government in Louisiana and Arkansas. . . .

Congress Has Been Deprived of Its Powers

Even the President's proclamation of the 8th of December formally declares that "whether members sent to Congress from any State shall be admitted to seats constitutionally rests exclusively with the respective houses, and not to any extent with the executive." And that is not the less true, because wholly inconsistent with the President's assumption, in that proclamation, of a right to institute and recognize State governments in the rebel States, nor because the President is unable to perceive that his recognition is a nullity if it be not conclusive upon Congress.

Under the Constitution, the right to senators and representatives is inseparable from a State government. If there be a State government, the right is absolute. If there be no State government, there can be no senators or representatives chosen. The two houses of Congress are expressly declared to be the sole judges of their own members. When, therefore, senators and representatives are admitted, the State government under whose authority they were chosen is conclusively established; when they are rejected, its existence is as conclusively rejected and denied. And to this judgment the President is bound to submit. . . .

A more studied outrage on the legislative authority of the people has never been perpetrated. Congress passed a bill, the President refused to approve it; and then, by proclamation, puts as much of it in force as he sees fit, and proposes to execute those parts by officers unknown to the laws of the United States and not subject to the confirmation of the Senate. . . . The bill provided for the civil administration of the laws of the State till it should be in a fit temper to govern itself, repealing all laws recognizing slavery, and making all men equal before the law. These beneficent provisions the President has annulled. People will die, and marry, and transfer property, and buy and sell, and to these acts of civil life courts and officers of the law are necessary. Congress legislated for these necessary things, and the President deprives them of the protection of the law. The President's purpose to instruct his military governors to "proceed according to the bill"—a make-shift to calm the disappointment its defeat has occasioned—is not merely a grave usurpation, but a transparent delusion. He can not "proceed according to the bill" after preventing it from becoming a law. Whatever is done will be at his will and pleasure, by persons responsible to no law, and more interested to secure the interests and execute the will of the President than of the people, and the will of Congress is to be "held for naught," unless "the loyal people of the rebel States choose to adopt it. . . ."

It was the solemn resolve of Congress to protect the loyal men of the nation against three great dangers: (1) the return to power of the guilty leaders of the rebellion; (2) the continuance of slavery; and (3) the burden of the rebel debt. Congress required assent to those provisions of the Convention of the State and, if refused, it was to be dissolved. The President "holds for naught" that resolve of Congress, because he is unwilling "to be inflexibly committed to any one plan of restoration"; and the people of the United States are not to be allowed to protect themselves unless their enemies agree to it. The order to proceed according to the bill is therefore merely at the will of the rebel States, and they have the option to reject it and accept the proclamation of the 8th of December, and demand the President's recognition. Mark the contrast! The bill requires a majority, the proclamation is satisfied with one tenth; the bill requires one oath, the proclamation another; the bill ascertains votes by registering, the proclamation by guess; the bill extracts adherence to existing territorial limits, the proclamation admits of others; the bill governs the rebel States *by law*, equalizing all before it, the proclamation commits them to the lawless discretion of military governors and provost-marshals; the bill forbids electors for President, the proclamation and defeat of the bill threaten us with civil war for the admission or exclusion of such votes; the bill exacted exclusion of dangerous enemies from power, and the relief of the nation from the rebel debt, and the prohibition of slavery forever, so that the suppression of the rebellion will double our resources to bear or pay the national debt, free the masses from the old domination of the rebel leaders, and eradicate the cause of the war; the proclamation secures neither of these guarantees.

An Illegal Oath

It is silent respecting the rebel debt and the political exclusion of rebel leaders, leaving slavery exactly where it was by law at the outbreak of the rebellion, and adds no guarantees even of the freedom of the slaves the President undertook to manumit. It is summed up in an illegal oath, without a sanction, and therefore void. The oath is to support all proclamations of the President during the rebellion having reference to slaves. Any government is to be accepted at the hands of one tenth of the people not contravening that oath. Now that oath neither secures the abolition of slavery, nor adds any security to the freedom of the slaves whom the President declared free. It does not secure the abolition of slavery, for the proclamation of freedom merely professed to free certain slaves, while it recognized the institution. Every Constitution of the rebel States at the outbreak of the rebellion may be adopted, without the change of a letter, for none of them contravene that proclamation, none of them *establish* slavery. . . .

The President has greatly presumed on the forbearance which the supporters of his administration have so long practiced, in view of the arduous conflict in which we are engaged, and the reckless ferocity of our political opponents.

But he must understand that our support is of a cause, and not of man; that the authority of Congress is paramount, and must be respected; that the whole body of the Union men of Congress will not submit to be impeached by him of rash and unconstitutional legislation; and if he wishes our support, he must confine himself to his executive duties—to obey and execute—not to make the laws; to suppress by arms armed rebellion, and leave political reorganization to the Congress.

Viewpoint 3

"[The people of the Confederacy] deliberately renounced their allegiance to the Federal Government, and proceeded to establish an independent government for themselves."

The South Is a Separate, Conquered Nation

The Joint Committee on Reconstruction

In December 1865 Congress established the Joint Committee on Reconstruction. The committee's fifteen members investigated the condition of the postwar South and made recommendations for all reconstruction bills. The agenda of the committee was shaped heavily by Senator Thaddeus Stevens, a Republican who supported Radical Reconstruction, a plan that advocated the complete overhaul of southern society. In the following excerpt from the committee's report, the majority (Republican) members argue that the South is a separate and conquered nation and therefore is not entitled to congressional representation or constitutional guarantees. This argument had far-reaching implications, the most important of which was that without rights, the southern states could be treated as the Radical Republicans saw fit.

The Joint Committee on Reconstruction, "Part 3," *Report of the Joint Committee on Reconstruction*, 39th Congress, 1st Session, 1866.

A claim for the immediate admission of Senators and Representatives from the so-called Confederate States has been urged, which seems to your committee not to be founded either in reason or in law, and which cannot be passed without comment. Stated in a few words, it amounts to this: That inasmuch as the lately insurgent States had no legal right to separate themselves from the Union, they still retain their positions as States, and consequently the people thereof have a right to immediate representation in Congress without the imposition of any conditions whatever; and further, that until such admission Congress has no right to tax them for the support of the Government. It has even been contended that until such admission all legislation affecting their interests is, if not unconstitutional, at least unjustifiable and oppressive.

It is believed by your committee that all these propositions are not only wholly untenable, but, if admitted, would tend to the destruction of the Government.

An Unjustified Rebellion

It must not be forgotten that the people of these States, without justification or excuse, rose in insurrection against the United States. They deliberately abolished their State governments so far as the same connected them politically with the Union as members thereof under the Constitution. They deliberately renounced their allegiance to the Federal Government, and proceeded to establish an independent government for themselves. In the prosecution of this enterprise they seized the national forts, arsenals, dockyards, and other public property within their borders, drove out from among them those who remained true to the Union, and heaped every imaginable insult and injury upon the United States and its citizens. Finally they opened hostilities, and levied war against the Government.

They continued this war for four years with the most determined and malignant spirit, killing in battle and otherwise large numbers of loyal people, destroying the property of loyal citizens on the sea and on the land, and entailing on the Government an enormous debt, incurred to sustain its rightful authority. Whether legally and constitutionally or not, they did, in fact, withdraw from the Union and made themselves subjects of another government of their own creation. And they only yielded when, after a long, bloody, and wasting war, they were compelled by utter exhaustion to lay down their arms; and this they did not willingly, but declaring that they yielded because they could no longer resist, affording no evidence whatever of repentance for their crime, and expressing no regret, except that they had no longer the power to continue the desperate struggle.

It cannot, we think, be denied by anyone, having a tolerable acquaintance with public law, that the war thus waged was a civil war of the greatest magnitude. The people waging it were necessarily subject to all the rules which, by the law of nations, control a contest of that character, and to all the legitimate consequences following it. One of those consequences was that, within the limits prescribed by humanity, the conquered rebels were at the mercy of the conquerors. That a government thus outraged had a most perfect right to exact indemnity for the injuries done and security against the recurrence of such outrages in the future would seem too clear for dispute. What the nature of that security should be, what proof should be required of a return to allegiance, what time should elapse before a people thus demoralized should be restored in full to the enjoyment of political rights and privileges, are questions for the law-making power to decide, and

The United States at the Beginning of the Civil War

Free States
Slave States
Free Areas That Later Allowed Slavery

that decision must depend on grave considerations of the public safety and the general welfare.

It is moreover contended, and with apparent gravity, that, from the peculiar nature and character of our Government, no such right on the part of the conqueror can exist; that from the moment when rebellion lays down its arms and actual hostilities cease, all political rights of rebellious communities are at once restored; that, because the people of a State of the Union were once an organized community within the Union, they necessarily so remain, and their right to be represented in Congress at any and all times, and to participate in the government of the country under all circumstances, admits of neither question or dispute. If this is indeed true, then is the Government of the United States powerless for its own protection, and flagrant rebellion, carried to the extreme of civil war, is a pastime which any State may play at, not only certain that it can lose nothing in any event, but may even be the gainer by defeat. If rebellion succeeds, it accomplishes its purpose and destroys the Government. If it fails, the war has been barren of results, and the battle may be still fought out in the legislative halls of the country. Treason, defeated in the field, has only to take possession of Congress and the cabinet. . . .

We now purpose to re-state, as briefly as possible, the general facts and principles applicable to all the States recently in rebellion.

First. The seats of the senators and representatives from the so-called Confederate States became vacant in the year 1861, during the second session of the Thirty-sixth Congress, by the voluntary withdrawal of their incumbents, with the sanction and by direction of the legislatures or conventions of their respective States. This was done as a hostile act against the Constitution and Government of the United States, with a declared intent to overthrow the same by forming a southern confederation. This act of declared hostility was speedily followed by an organization of the same States into a confederacy, which levied and waged war, by sea and land, against the United States. This war continued more than four years, within which period the rebel armies besieged the national capital, invaded the loyal States, burned their towns and cities, robbed their citizens, destroyed more than 250,000 loyal soldiers, and imposed an increased national burden of not less than

$3,500,000,000, of which seven or eight hundred millions have already been met and paid. From the time these confederated States thus withdrew their representation in Congress and levied war against the United States, the great mass of their people became and were insurgents, rebels, traitors, and all of them assumed and occupied the political, legal, and practical relation of enemies of the United States. This position is established by acts of Congress and judicial decisions, and is recognized repeatedly by the President in public proclamations, documents, and speeches.

Second. The States thus confederated prosecuted their war against the United States to final arbitrament, and did not cease until all their armies were captured, their military powers destroyed, their civil officers, State and confederate, taken prisoners or put to flight, every vestige of State and confederate government obliterated, their territory overrun and occupied by the federal armies, and their people reduced to the condition of enemies conquered in war, entitled only by public law to such rights, privileges, and conditions as might be vouchsafed by the conqueror. . . .

Sixth. The question before Congress is, then, whether conquered enemies have the right, and shall be permitted at their own pleasure and on their own terms, to participate in making laws for their conquerors; whether conquered rebels may change their theater of operations from the battle-field, where they were defeated and overthrown, to the halls of Congress, and, through their representatives, seize upon the Government which they fought to destroy; whether the national treasury, the army of the nation, its navy, its forts and arsenals, its whole civil administration, its credit, its pensioners, the widows and orphans of those who perished in the war, the public honor, peace and safety, shall all be turned over to the keeping of its recent enemies without delay, and without imposing such conditions as, in the opinion of Congress, the security of the country and its institutions may demand.

Seventh. The history of mankind exhibits no example of such madness and folly. The instinct of self-preservation protests against it.

Viewpoint 4

"It is clear to my apprehension that the States lately in rebellion are still members of the National Union."

The South Is Not a Separate, Conquered Nation

Andrew Johnson

When Abraham Lincoln was re-elected in 1864, his running mate, Andrew Johnson—the only southern senator who supported the Union during the Civil War—became vice president. However, he was vice president for only a few weeks before Lincoln was assassinated, after which he became the seventeenth president of the United States.

Johnson's presidency was marked by a struggle with Congress over reconstruction. In particular, the executive and legislative branches argued over the status of the former Confederate states. In his State of the Union address of December 1867, excerpted below, Johnson contends that the southern states should not be considered a separate nation. According to the president, during the war the South was a rebellious faction, not a hostile nation. Therefore, because the southern states had never been separated from the Union, they could not be denied basic constitutional rights and representation during reconstruction.

Andrew Johnson, State of the Union Address, December 3, 1867.

When a civil war has been brought to a close, it is manifestly the first interest and duty of the state to repair the injuries which the war has inflicted, and to secure the benefit of the lessons it teaches as fully and as speedily as possible. This duty was, upon the termination of the rebellion, promptly accepted, not only by the executive department, but by the insurrectionary States themselves, and restoration in the first moment of peace was believed to be as easy and certain as it was indispensable. The expectations, however, then so reasonably and confidently entertained were disappointed by legislation from which I felt constrained by my obligations to the Constitution to withhold my assent.

It is therefore a source of profound regret that in complying with the obligation imposed upon the President by the Constitution to give to Congress from time to time information of the state of the Union I am unable to communicate any definitive adjustment, satisfactory to the American people, of the questions which since the close of the rebellion have agitated the public mind. On the contrary, candor compels me to declare that at this time there is no Union as our fathers understood the term, and as they meant it to be understood by us. The Union which they established can exist only where all the States are represented in both Houses of Congress; where one State is as free as another to regulate its internal concerns according to its own will, and where the laws of the central Government, strictly confined to matters of national jurisdiction, apply with equal force to all the people of every section. That such is not the present "state of the Union" is a melancholy fact, and we must all acknowledge that the restoration of the States to their proper legal relations with the Federal Government and with one another, according to the terms of the original compact, would be the greatest temporal blessing which God, in His kindest providence, could bestow upon this nation. It becomes our imperative duty to consider whether or not it is impossible to effect this most desirable consummation.

The Union and the Constitution are inseparable. As long as one is obeyed by all parties, the other will be preserved; and if one is destroyed, both must perish together. The destruction of the Constitution will be followed by other and still greater calamities. It was ordained not only to form a more perfect union between the

States, but to "establish justice, insure domestic tranquility, provide for the common defense, promote the general welfare, and secure the blessings of liberty to ourselves and our posterity." Nothing but implicit obedience to its requirements in all parts of the country will accomplish these great ends. Without that obedience we can look forward only to continual outrages upon individual rights, incessant breaches of the public peace, national weakness, financial dishonor, the total loss of our prosperity, the general corruption of morals, and the final extinction of popular freedom. To save our country from evils so appalling as these, we should renew our efforts again and again.

To me the process of restoration seems perfectly plain and simple. It consists merely in a faithful application of the Constitution and laws. The execution of the laws is not now obstructed or opposed by physical force. There is no military or other necessity, real or pretended, which can prevent obedience to the Constitution, either North or South. All the rights and all the obligations of States and individuals can be protected and enforced by means perfectly consistent with the fundamental law. The courts may be everywhere open, and if open their process would be unimpeded. Crimes against the United States can be prevented or punished by the proper judicial authorities in a manner entirely practicable and legal. There is therefore no reason why the Constitution should not be obeyed, unless those who exercise its powers have determined that it shall be disregarded and violated. The mere naked will of this Government, or of some one or more of its branches, is the only obstacle that can exist to a perfect union of all the States. . . .

It is clear to my apprehension that the States lately in rebellion are still members of the National Union. When did they cease to be so? The "ordinances of secession" adopted by a portion (in most of them a very small portion) of their citizens were mere nullities. If we admit now that they were valid and effectual for the purpose intended by their authors, we sweep from under our feet the whole ground upon which we justified the war. Were those States afterwards expelled from the Union by the war? The direct contrary was averred by this Government to be its purpose, and was so understood by all those who gave their blood and treasure to aid in its prosecution. It cannot be that a successful war, waged for the preservation of the Union, had the legal effect of dissolving it. The victory of the nation's arms was not the disgrace of her

---

The State of Loyalty in the South

Journalist Benjamin C. Truman traveled throughout the Deep South from September 1865 to March 1866 as an official emissary of President Johnson. Upon his return to the North, Truman presented his observations in a speech before Congress. In his testimony, which has been excerpted below, Truman asserts that while southerners are not uniform in their attitudes, the former rebellious states are displaying increasing loyalty toward the federal government.

Though there is no district in Florida that can strictly be called loyal in contradistinction to all others, yet I found the feeling of the people in that State much better and more encouraging than in Georgia, which is overrun with politicians, many of whom seem to defy the government and its authority. Alabama is in a much better condition than Georgia, and its state of affairs is extremely encouraging. Mississippi, from one end to the other, of all the States which I visited, is far behindhand in her tokens of loyalty; there is an unmistakable flow of ill feeling in that State, although I witnessed no exhibitions of unmitigated disloyalty; on the whole, the people of that State fear the authority of the United States more than they respect it. In Louisiana there is an encouraging element of loyalty which is experiencing a healthy increase. Tennessee evidenced in a great degree the most flourishings signs of loyalty; I do not think there are ten men in that State at present who could be induced to favor a dissolution of the Union, not even indeed, if such a thing should be peaceably permitted. There is a healthy intercourse between all classes in Arkansas, and it seemed to me to occupy nearly the identical position of Tennessee.

Benjamin C. Truman, testimony before the Senate, 1866.

policy; the defeat of secession on the battlefield was not the triumph of its lawless principle. Nor could Congress, with or without the consent of the Executive, do anything which would have the effect, directly or indirectly, of separating the States from each other. To dissolve the Union is to repeal the Constitution which holds it together, and that is a power which does not belong to any department of this Government, or to all of them united.

The Supremity of the Constitution

This is so plain that it has been acknowledged by all branches of the Federal Government. The Executive (my predecessor as well as myself) and the heads of all the Departments have uniformly acted upon the principle that the Union is not only undissolved, but indissoluble. Congress submitted an amendment of the Constitution to be ratified by the Southern States, and accepted their acts of ratification as a necessary and lawful exercise of their highest function. If they were not States, or were States out of the Union, their consent to a change in the fundamental law of the Union would have been nugatory, and Congress in asking it committed a political absurdity. The judiciary has also given the solemn sanction of its authority to the same view of the case. The judges of the Supreme Court have included the Southern States in their circuits, and they are constantly, *in banc* and elsewhere, exercising jurisdiction which does not belong to them unless those States are States of the Union.

If the Southern States are component parts of the Union, the Constitution is the supreme law for them, as it is for all the other States. They are bound to obey it, and so are we. The right of the Federal Government, which is clear and unquestionable, to enforce the Constitution upon them implies the correlative obligation on our part to observe its limitations and execute its guaranties. Without the Constitution we are nothing; by, through, and under the Constitution we are what it makes us. We may doubt the wisdom of the law, we may not approve of its provisions, but we can not violate it merely because it seems to confine our powers within limits narrower than we could wish. It is not a question of individual or class or sectional interest, much less of party predominance, but of duty—of high and sacred duty—which we are all sworn to perform. If we can not support the Constitution with the cheerful alacrity of those who love and believe in it, we must give to it as least the fidelity of public servants who act under solemn obligations and commands which they dare not disregard.

The constitutional duty is not the only one which requires the States to be restored. There is another consideration which, though of minor importance, is yet of great weight. On the 22d day of July, 1861, Congress declared by an almost unanimous vote of both Houses that the war should be condemned solely for the purpose of preserving the Union and maintaining the supremacy of the Federal Constitution and laws, without impairing the dignity, equality, and rights of the States or of individuals, and that when this was done the war should cease. I do not say that this declaration is personally binding on those who joined in making it, any more than individual members of Congress are personally bound to pay a public debt created under a law for which they voted. But it was a solemn, public, official pledge of the national honor, and I cannot imagine upon what grounds the repudiation of it is to be justified. If it be said that we are not bound to keep faith with rebels, let it be remembered that this promise was not made to rebels only. Thousands of true men in the South were drawn to our standard by it, and hundreds of thousands in the North gave their lives in the belief that it would be carried out. It was made on the day after the first great battle of the war had been fought and lost. All patriotic and intelligent men then saw the necessity of giving such an assurance, and believed that without it the war would end in disaster to our cause. Having given that assurance in the extremity of our peril, the violation of it now, in the day of our power, would be a rude rending of that good faith which holds the moral world together; our country would cease to have any claim upon the confidence of men; it would make the war not only a failure, but a fraud. . . .

Punishments Must Be Reasonable

I have no desire to save from the proper and just consequences of their great crime those who engaged in rebellion against the Government, but as a mode of punishment the measures under consideration are the most unreasonable that could be invented. Many of those people are perfectly innocent; many kept their fidelity to the Union untainted to the last; many were incapable of any legal offense; a large proportion even of the persons able to bear arms were forced into rebellion against their will, and of those who are guilty with their own consent the degrees of guilt are as various as the shades of their character and temper. But these acts of Congress confound them all together in one common doom. Indiscriminate vengeance upon classes, sects, and parties, or upon whole communities, for offenses committed by a portion of them against the governments to which they owed obedience was common in the barbarous ages of the world; but Christianity and civilization have made such progress that recourse to a punishment so cruel and unjust would meet with the condemnation of all unprejudiced and right-minded men. The punitive justice of this age, and especially of this country, does not consist in stripping whole States of their liberties and reducing all their people, without distinction, to the condition of slavery. It deals separately with each individual, confines itself to the forms of law, and vindicates its own purity by an impartial examination of every case before a competent judicial tribunal. If this does not satisfy all our desires with regard to Southern rebels, let us console ourselves by reflecting that a free Constitution, triumphant in war and unbroken in peace, is worth far more to us and our children than the gratification of any present feeling.

I am aware it is assumed that this system of government for the Southern States is not to be perpetual. It is true this military government is to be only provisional, but it is through this temporary evil that a greater evil is to be made perpetual. If the guaranties of the Constitution can be broken provisionally to serve a temporary purpose, and in a part only of the country, we can destroy them everywhere and for all time. Arbitrary measures often change, but they generally change for the worse. It is the curse of despotism that has no halting place. The intermitted exercise of its power brings no sense of security to its subjects, for they can never know what more they will be called to endure when its red right hand is armed to plague them again. Nor is it possible to conjecture how or where power, unrestrained by law, may seek its next victims. The States that are still free may be enslaved at any moment; for if the Constitution does not protect all, it protects none.

Viewpoint 5

"[President Abraham] Lincoln moved . . . ahead of northern opinion, not to mention white American opinion in general."

Lincoln's Reconstruction Plan Contained Some Elements of Radicalism

Gabor S. Boritt

As the Civil War progressed and it became increasingly clear that the Union army would triumph, President Lincoln began developing plans for reconstructing the nation. Two templates for reconstruction battled for the president's attention: the radical approach, which posited that the seceded states were now conquered territories, and the conservative plan, under which the seceded areas retained their statehood. At the center of this debate was slavery. If the radical point of view prevailed, Congress would be able to abolish slavery in Southern states; however, if the conservative plan were implemented, the federal government would not have the constitutional authority to free slaves in the Southern states.

In the following selection Gabor S. Boritt contends that Lincoln's blueprint for reconstruction contained some radical elements. According to Boritt, the president supported the Radical Republicans by demanding the emancipation of slaves in the conquered Southern states and by stating that blacks who were educated, owned property, or had served in the Union army should be given the right to vote. The president and Republican-led Congress also worked together on issues such as the abolition of slavery in the District of Columbia and the admittance of West Virginia as a free state. However, as Boritt explains, Lincoln did not want to alienate centrist voters during the 1864 presidential election and thus vetoed the Wade-Davis Bill, which had elements of Radicalism and would have made Congress a more integral player in the reconstruction process. The president also struggled to gain Radical support during his rebuilding of Louisiana's government. Ultimately Lincoln's plans would be thwarted by his assassination in April 1865. Boritt is the director of the Civil War Institute and the Fluhrer Professor of Civil War Studies at Gettysburg College in Pennsylvania.

Emancipation . . . was a central step in reconstructing the United States. The war had begun with the announced goal of restoring the Union as it was in 1860. In 1861, surely by 1862, the goal had shifted toward Reconstruction, the reshaping of the Union without slavery. As the war continued and then veered toward a close, a further shift occurred, expanding the goal of the struggle to include union, emancipation, and movement toward civil rights for the freedman. The interplays between the North and the South, between factions in both, and between Congress and the executive in Washington were complex, but the central issue remained the role of African Americans in American society. Lincoln moved behind a radical vanguard but ahead of northern opinion, not to mention white American opinion in general and at times ahead of the consensus of his Republican party as well. The question to him was not "'Can any of us imagine better?' but 'Can we all do better?'" With this clear, pragmatic motto before him, he led Americans toward acceptance of ever greater black freedom.

The president consistently refused to recognize the validity of secession ordinances and, in legal terms, looked upon the Union as an unbroken and unbreakable unit. The war constituted a set of problems that he, as commander in chief, had to deal with, and Reconstruction measures fell into this category of problems. At the same time, he was ready to allow Congress a substantial and constitutionally legitimate role in the Reconstruction process.

President Lincoln's Plan

In the middle of 1863, as parts of Arkansas, Louisiana, Texas, Florida, Virginia, and all of Tennessee came under the control of federal arms, Lincoln brought into being local military governments. Their chief task was to rally southern Unionists, subdue and keep away rebels and their sympathizers, and bring about a new day for blacks.

At the end of 1863 the president proposed his Proclamation of Amnesty and Reconstruction. It included the "10 Percent Plan"—well received in Congress—which called for the formation of civilian governments when one-tenth of the voting population of 1860 took the oath of allegiance to the United States. Emancipation was not to be open for discussion in these states. Many citizens were proscribed from participation in the political process either as voters or officeholders: individuals who had held diplomatic or civil posts in the Confederacy, Confederate officers above the rank of colonel, those who had resigned from the armed forces of the United States or from any branches of the government, and those who had mistreated federal prisoners of war. His proposal notwithstanding, Lincoln insisted that flexibility should be the key to Reconstruction and that different plans might be needed in different times and places.

Louisiana became Lincoln's test case. Initially he had overestimated southern unionism there, as elsewhere in the South. When satisfactory Reconstruction failed to materialize, he increasingly involved himself in personally directing the Louisiana experiment.

His style combined daring, strength, and coercion with caution, conciliation, and ambiguity. It demanded movement, but only step by step, and entailed the use of patronage, the military, and other tools of presidential power. It included a precise, lawyerly command of the language, a unique eloquence, and a genius for ambiguity. This last quality, though needed, helped confuse many Radicals in Congress (and later historians as well). The president created a government, under General Nathaniel P. Banks, that struck down slavery, provided for public schools for blacks and whites, and empowered the state legislature to enfranchise blacks. As white Louisiana Unionists faced the hostile pro-Confederate majority, Lincoln labored with finesse to keep the former united—hence, much of his ambiguity. Yet, as early as August 1863, Lincoln was ready to have the color line on the franchise breached. In March 1864 he wrote his famous letter to Governor Michael Hahn calling for voting rights for "very intelligent" blacks and black veterans because "they could probably help, in some trying time to come, to keep the jewel of liberty within the family of freedom." Rather than being a mere suggestion for "private consideration," this was a "directive," as historian LaWanda Cox has shown, and was understood as such by Louisiana leaders. In short, Lincoln led the Unionists toward black suffrage while pretending to stay in the background.

Ironically, the Radicals in Washington tried to strike down the Louisiana free-state movement in the name of black suffrage and Lincoln's abuse of military power. The conflict that then developed between the executive and the legislature sometimes overshadowed the cooperation between the two, not merely in various areas of governmental work but specifically on Reconstruction. Lincoln had, after all, worked well with Congress to abolish slavery in the territories and the District of Columbia; to admit West Virginia, split off from Virginia, as a new free state; and to smooth out disagreements over the 1862 Confiscation Act.[1] And they would later work together in establishing the Freedmen's Bureau

1. Passed on July 17, 1862, the Confiscation Act declared that slaves who were owned by Confederate officials in Southern states occupied by the Union army, "shall be forever free."

to help care for the freed slaves and, most momentously, in pushing through Congress the Thirteenth Amendment, thereby abolishing slavery under the Constitution. Nonetheless, early in 1864,
Lincoln provoked a split with the Radicals. Congressman Henry
Winter Davis of Maryland and Senator Benjamin F. Wade of Ohio
produced a somewhat muddled bill in favor of congressional Reconstruction. Though the bill did not call for black suffrage, it had
the aura of Radicalism about it. Lincoln pocket vetoed the bill—
the only important veto of his presidency—much less because of
the larger issues of Reconstruction than because of the upcoming
presidential election. While the Wade-Davis bill had wound its
way through Congress, the president had remained silent. Then,
to the surprise of many, including his friends in Congress, he declined to sign the measure. Probably many of his friends would
have refused to support the Wade-Davis bill if they had known his
position. As correspondent Noah Brooks summed it up in *Washington in Lincoln's Time* (1895), it was only when the executive
acted that "for the first time men who had not seriously opposed
the passage of the . . . bill began to wish that it had never gone to
the President." It seems that Lincoln wanted the opportunity to
veto the bill and draw a sharp line between himself and the Radicals. A few days earlier, equally surprisingly but to the same effect,
he accepted the resignation of [Salmon] Chase, the resident Radical of the cabinet. But then, elections are usually won at the center, and Lincoln did win. Soon after he was quite ready to accept
more than the Wade-Davis policy for Reconstruction and appoint
Chase chief justice of the United States.

Political and Economic Freedoms

Lincoln was intent on seeing his Louisiana experiment through
but also hoped to work with the Radicals. He had played a crucial
role in the adoption of the Thirteenth Amendment by a somewhat
reluctant House of Representatives. In his last public address, on
11 April [1865], before the White House, he pleaded for saving
the Louisiana government that congressional Radicals opposed:
"Concede that the new government of Louisiana is only to what
it should be as the egg is to the fowl, we shall sooner have the fowl
by hatching the egg than by smashing it."

What the fowl was to look like he indicated by expressing his personal preference for giving the franchise to blacks who were educated, or propertied, or were Union veterans. How far he was to go beyond that, or with what speed, we do not know, but his course would have depended in no small part on what he judged to be attainable. The direction he took was clear, and though he knew each state to be unique, in his last address he also explained that "what has been said of Louisiana will apply to other states."

Lincoln knew and prized the achievement of black soldiers against heavy odds, which he could not always readily lighten. As early as 1863, he had spoken glowingly of the black man who "with silent tongue, and clenched teeth, and steady eye, and well-poised bayonet, . . . helped mankind" to the great consummation of freedom. Blacks had fought in more than 190 battles, and about 68,000 black soldiers and sailors had been killed or wounded. Twenty one blacks won the Congressional Medal of Honor. A black regiment was the first to march into Richmond when the Confederate capital fell, and Lincoln toured the city escorted by black cavalry. No one could misunderstand the significance of his escort. For the postwar era Lincoln was determined to bring both political and economic advancement to blacks.

His commitment to black freedom fit into a larger commitment to a democratic, capitalist America. And so his postwar response to black needs would have also depended in no small part on his response to the coming Gilded Age.[2]

Reconstruction for Lincoln meant more than providing a place for blacks in "a new birth of freedom," central though that issue was. He was also concerned with southern whites, even the former slaveholder, and as late as 1865, he gave serious attention to compensating slaveholders. During the war years his numerous peace feelers and reconstruction schemes included strong appeals to the economic interests of the Confederates. He assumed, somewhat naively for a time of bitter war, that materialist enticements could seduce the South into peace. This assumption largely explains the absurdly vast amount of time he devoted to the prob-

---

2. the two-decade period following the Civil War that was marked by Republican corruption, including questionable dealings with oil barons

lems of trading with the Confederacy (the corruption it bred notwithstanding), especially in cotton. The same was true of his secret feelers about the federal takeover of the Confederate war debt (obliquely attacked in the Wade-Davis Manifesto), his persistent offers for large-scale compensation for slaves, his lack of enthusiasm for congressional laws of confiscation, and perhaps even the unrealistic presidential request that the Pacific Railroad be built on the five-foot gauge used primarily in the South. After the war ended, such economic incentives were likely to have more substantial effects. The blueprint that Congress created during the war for a modern nation was also a blueprint for the new, reconstructed America. . . .

Lincoln's Hopes

In March 1865, at his second inaugural, Lincoln delivered another speech that might be described as one of the finest in the English language. He again looked ahead:

> Fondly do we hope, fervently do we pray, that this mighty scourge of war may speedily pass away. . . . With malice toward none, with charity for all, . . . let us strive on to finish the work we are in, to bind up the nation's wounds, . . . to do all which may achieve and cherish a just and lasting peace among ourselves and with all nations.

Six weeks later, on the night of 14 April 1865, Good Friday, the president was shot while attending a performance at Ford's Theater in Washington. He died nine hours later. He thus did not live to see how difficult it would be to create a "new life," a "new birth of freedom," in a new America.

Viewpoint 6

"[Lincoln] was too conservative to satisfy the deep but as yet unexpressed demands of his party for 'security' and 'repentance.'"

Lincoln's Reconstruction Plan Was Too Conservative

Avery Craven

By the middle of 1863, the Union army occupied Tennessee, Louisiana, and North Carolina. As it became apparent that the North would triumph in the Civil War, Abraham Lincoln began developing a plan to bring the conquered areas back into the United States. His 10 Percent Plan required that seceded states obtain an oath of allegiance to the United States from 10 percent of the voters before they would be admitted back into the Union.

In the following viewpoint Avery Craven argues that Lincoln's efforts at reconstruction failed because the 10 Percent Plan was too conservative. In Lincoln's mind, while the southern states had seceded from the Union, they had never lost their statehood or the rights that attended their status. Thus, Lincoln did not believe that Congress had the constitutional authority to dictate

Avery Craven, *Reconstruction: The Ending of the Civil War.* New York: Holt, Rinehart and Winston, 1969. Copyright © 1969 by Holt, Rinehart and Winston, Inc. All rights reserved. Reproduced by permission of the author.

to the southern states on matters concerning slavery. Craven contends that in consequence, Lincoln's proposal did not improve social and economic conditions for former slaves or force southerners to change their views on race and class. Craven was a historian and professor who wrote several books on the Civil War and Reconstruction, including *Reconstruction: The Ending of the Civil War*, from which this selection has been excerpted.

As the war was coming to an end, Lincoln began experimenting with his plan for quick reconstruction. In southern states where federal troops had established a firm foothold, he appointed military governors who were to encourage and organize Union sentiment and bring loyal governments into being under his 10 percent proposal. In this way he soon had military governors at work in Tennessee, Arkansas, and Louisiana. He had no final, fixed program; he was just experimenting. He told his officials in Louisiana, which was to serve as a test case, to follow the forms of law as far as convenient, but at all events to get the expression of loyalty from the largest number of people possible. The situation was, he said, "so new and unprecedented . . . that no exclusive and inflexible plan can be prescribed as to details and collaterals."

So uncertain was Lincoln of the final course to be followed that he frankly said that if any loyal southern state wished to follow the Wade-Davis procedure[1] (which he had pocket-vetoed), he would be "fully satisfied." He evidently would have one plan for one state, a different plan for another state, as practical circumstances dictated.

Any attempt to echo what was in Lincoln's mind is, of course, only conjecture. As an astute politician, he may have realized that his party had been, and probably still would be, a minority party when the nation resumed a normal course. By a quick and generous restoration of the southern states, he may have been aiming at the building of a southern Republican wing on old Whig foundations. He may have been only expressing the deep human qual-

1. The Wade-Davis Bill was proposed by Radical Republicans and would have required seceded states' new governments to repudiate secession and abolish slavery.

ities which were part of a man to whom war had brought much of sorrow but little of hatred.

The Process Begins

At any rate, under his 10 percent plan reconstruction in Louisiana proceeded rapidly. The test oath was administered, a convention was called, a constitution was formed prohibiting slavery, and a governor and United States senators were chosen. Internal affairs were left largely to the people, yet Lincoln suggested to Governor Michael Hahn that the vote be given to qualified Negroes. He noted that only the United States Senate had the right to decide on the admission of the Louisiana senators. This matter was, therefore, referred to the Senate Judiciary Committee. On February 17, 1865 its chairman, Lyman Trumbull, reported a joint resolution: "That the United States do hereby recognize the government of the State of Louisiana as a legitimate government of the said state and entitled to the guarantees and all other rights of a State Government under the Constitution of the United States."

Abolitionist Charles Sumner, who had been demanding the vote for all Negroes, bitterly opposed this resolution and started a filibuster to prevent its adoption. Caught with the necessity of passing an army and navy bill, the Senate yielded and the resolution was set aside. Louisiana would have to wait.

After much confusion and uncertainty, both Tennessee and Arkansas also held conventions and framed constitutions abolishing slavery and repudiating secession. The government of Virginia under Francis Harrison Pierpont was recognized as the legitimate government of that state. With Lincoln's death and with growing resistance in Congress, none of these three states was admitted. Further steps toward reconstruction thus fell to President Andrew Johnson, who came from a state not yet a member of the Union. It should be noted that many who had opposed Lincoln's southern experiments welcomed Johnson's accession to the Presidency. They agreed with Indiana Senator George W. Julian that Lincoln's removal "would prove a godsend to the country." They had already met to urge a new cabinet and "a line of policy less conciliatory" than that of Mr. Lincoln, "whose tenderness to the Rebels" and views on reconstruction were as "distasteful as possible."

Lincoln's Complete Failure

Historians have generally been reluctant to evaluate Lincoln's reconstruction efforts. They were never brought to a final test, nor did they represent his final thinking on the whole subject. Yet even if we view Lincoln's efforts at reconstruction simply as experiments and not as parts of a well thought-out plan, one simple fact remains: although Lincoln had an efficient army to carry out his program, he failed completely.

Not a single state was brought back into the Union and the bitterness and confusion—both North and South—was increased. Granting Lincoln all the qualities of diplomacy, adroitness, and ability to get along with others, which supposedly would have prevented all that subsequently happened, he still failed to accomplish anything and, at the same time, created enemies in his own party who rejoiced at his death far more than did intelligent southerners.

Abraham Lincoln

Why did Lincoln fail so completely and why this angry opposition? The answer seems to lie in the fact that he was too conservative to satisfy the deep but as yet unexpressed demands of his party for "security" and "repentance." In his first message to Congress in December 1861, he had talked of compensation for states that freed their slaves. In his message of December 1, 1862, he had proposed an elaborate plan for ending the war by "delivering" interest-bearing government bonds to any state that would free its slaves, immediately or gradually, up to the first day of January 1900. In each case Lincoln favored colonizing the freed Negroes "at some place, or places, in a climate congenial to them." In his much-quoted letter of August 1864 to Charles D. Robinson (written but not sent), Lincoln reaffirmed his willingness to save the Union "without freeing any slave" if necessary. He then went on to assert that his statement that "reunion and abandonment of slavery would be considered, if offered" was not "saying that nothing *else* or *less* would be considered." He closed the letter by commenting that "if Jefferson Davis wishes, for himself, or for the benefit of his friends at the North, to know what I would do if he were to offer peace and re-union, saying nothing about slavery, let him try me."

All this was consistent with Lincoln's declaration that the war was being waged solely for the purpose of saving the Union. He held firmly to the constitutional theory that secession was impossible and that no southern state had ever been out of the Union. It had only been out of its "proper practical relation" to it. He had once said that he "thought the act of secession" was "legally nothing and needs no repealing." He had even been a bit lax about the loyalty oaths, advising one official to have the loyal as well as the disloyal take them because it "did not hurt them" and would swell the aggregate number required for this purpose. So when a reasonable number of the citizens of a state had taken the oath, incorporated into its constitution the fallacy of secession, accepted the abolition of slavery, perhaps given deserving Negroes the franchise and every chance for an education, renounced Confederate debts, and ratified the Thirteenth Amendment [abolishing slavery], it should resume its full rights as a state in the Union.

Lincoln Was Pragmatic

Two things in such a program were lacking. It did not provide adequate punishment for "unrepentant rebels," and it did not offer sufficient guaranty of justice and equality for the Negro. Lincoln had not learned to hate. He most certainly lagged far behind the "radical" element of his party in racial attitudes. He had seemingly accepted conditionally the existing system when he said that if the new state governments "recognized and declared [the freedmen's] permanent freedom, [and] provided for their education," the Executive would not object, "as a temporary arrangement," to "their present condition as a laboring, landless, and homeless class." Furthermore, he had earlier remarked that he did not favor "bringing about in any way the social and political equality of the white and black races . . . qualifying them to hold office, nor to intermarry with the white people. . . ." He had said repeatedly that he believed there were physical differences which would "forever forbid the two races living together on terms of social and political equality."

Lincoln had never in his own state attempted to remove the bar against Negroes voting, holding office, or attending the public schools. He had checked the army officers who had attempted to free the slaves in conquered areas, and, at all times, he had advocated the removal of the Negro, when freed, from the United States. He had never gone further than to say that slavery was morally wrong and that the Negro had a right to eat the bread his labor created. Lincoln would free him from slavery and grant him all the rights of a human being; but beyond that he conceded no plans for a social revolution. He had not even carried out the seizure of Confederate lands that the confiscation acts of 1861–1862 had authorized.

Nor had Lincoln required the southern people either to humiliate themselves or to undergo a complete social and intellectual revolution. He had ignored Congress, and, as the nation's executive, he had attempted to secure a quick return to normalcy in any state where conditions permitted. Lincoln's purpose was to put an end to bloodshed and to resume a national life. In other words, Lincoln had acted like a practical, pragmatic American politician taking what could intelligently be got. On the grounds that it was essential to maintain state identity in reconstruction, he even rejected War Secretary Edwin M. Stanton's proposal to combine Virginia and North Carolina into a single military district. As one critic wrote: "If there was a grievous fault in Mr. Lincoln's administration it was in the fostering of enemies, and the discarding of friends . . . in fattening rebels and starving those who had elevated him to power." This he thought had been carried to the point where rebellion had been made respectable. Lincoln had attempted the impossible. He had tried to run "the Train of Freedom with slavery conductors . . . giving them plenty of money if they would not smash the cars." The only true policy of government, he insisted, was "to the victors belong the control," and no man should be employed unless known "as the enemy of the rebellion." Only then would the nation be entirely safe.

CHAPTER 2

Conflicts During Reconstruction

Chapter Preface

Reconstruction was one of the most troubled eras in American history. Conflicts over how best to repair the war-torn nation drove wedges between northerners and southerners, Democrats and Republicans, and the president and Congress. The history of the Freedmen's Bureau, an agency established by Congress in March 1865, typifies these conflicts. Although the bureau aided the newly freed slaves in many ways, opposition from President Andrew Johnson and white southerners guaranteed that the bureau could not be wholly successful.

The purpose of the Freedmen's Bureau, known officially as the Bureau of Freedmen, Refugees, and Abandoned Property, was to help freedmen and Civil War refugees by offering a variety of services, including educational and medical services. However, in what would be the first sign that the Freedmen's Bureau's mission would not be an easy one, Congress decided not to appropriate any funds for the agency. As Robert Cruden explains in *The Negro in Reconstruction*, Congress believed "that income from sale or rental of confiscated Confederate federal property and of plantations seized by the Union army would meet the need of caring for millions of destitute whites and blacks." That plan was waylaid by President Johnson's decision to return confiscated lands to pardoned former Confederates. With insufficient funds to hire staff, the bureau turned to the army for employees. Unfortunately, as Cruden notes, many of these military men were corrupt and unsympathetic toward the freed blacks, making them wholly unsuited to work at the Bureau.

Other actions by Johnson suggested that he did not consider the Freedmen's bureau an essential element of reconstruction. A noteworthy example was his opposition to Lyman Trumbull's Freedmen Bureau's Bill of 1865. The bureau had originally been intended to last one year after the war ended, so Trumbull introduced his bill as a means of extending the life of the bureau, expanding its powers, and protecting "all persons in the United States in their civil rights." The bill passed in the Senate by a 37-

10 vote and in the House by a margin of 136-33. However, Johnson vetoed the bill, charging that it was an unconstitutional continuation of war powers. The Senate fell two votes short of the thirty-two needed to override the veto, but a revised bill passed in July 1866.

Johnson was not the only person who opposed the bureau. According to Cruden, many white planters and landowners were also hostile toward the bureau because of its efforts to provide land for freedmen and supervise contracts between white planters and black workers. Whites resented any interference on the part of bureau agents and believed the agents did not understand the true nature of southern race relations. Southern novelist Thomas Nelson Page, writing in the *Atlantic Monthly* in 1901, said of bureau officials: "All were absolutely ignorant of the true relation between the old masters and slaves; all had a bigoted people behind them, and a bigoted people before them." Page also contended that the bureau was wrong to think of the blacks as oppressed and the whites as tyrannical. The most virulent opposition came from the Ku Klux Klan. John Hope Franklin, in his book *Reconstruction: After the Civil War*, writes: "The attack on Bureau officials [by Klan members] was systematic and effective. Sometimes they were simply warned to leave town, sometimes they were flogged. . . . Even after the Bureau had been officially disbanded, former employees were marked objects of the wrath of the Klansmen."

Despite such opposition, the Freedmen's Bureau was not without accomplishments. Historian Martin Abbott declared the bureau a "limited success," observing that the bureau's agents helped blacks acquire land, protected them from white violence, and enabled the newly freed slaves to receive better wages and treatment than they would have managed on their own. In its first four years, the bureau also established more than forty hospitals and helped settle thirty thousand people who had been displaced by the war. In addition, the bureau suspended or overruled the more oppressive aspects of the Black Codes, laws passed by southern legislatures that placed a number of restrictions on blacks, including prohibiting them from serving on juries, intermarrying, or leasing or renting land in certain areas. However, the Freedmen's Bureau's greatest achievement was probably the establishment of an education system for freed blacks. By 1870 the Freedmen's Bureau had spent more than 5 million dollars on education, establishing 4,300 schools that taught approximately 250,000 blacks. In spite of these successes, the bureau was finally shuttered in 1872.

The history of the Freedmen's Bureau shows that the end of the war did not immediately translate into the beginning of peace. In the following chapter, authors examine other Reconstruction issues that pitted Americans against each other, making this era of American history one of the most turbulent.

Viewpoint 1

"Whatever law protects the white man shall afford 'equal' protection to the black man."

The Fourteenth Amendment Should Be Supported

Thaddeus Stevens

Pennsylvania representative Thaddeus Stevens was one of the leaders of the Radical Republicans, a powerful congressional faction that opposed presidential reconstruction. In 1866 Radical Republicans argued that a constitutional amendment was the only way to guarantee citizenship and equality for former slaves. The Joint Committee on Reconstruction—a fifteen-member committee established by Congress in December 1865 to study conditions in the South and make recommendations for reconstruction bills—responded to these concerns by drafting the Fourteenth Amendment.

In the following viewpoint, excerpted from a speech before the House of Representatives, Stevens argues in favor of the amendment. He contends that the amendment will correct unjust state laws and ensure that blacks will not receive harsher punishments than their white counterparts when they commit the same crimes. Stevens also maintains that the amendment will compel the southern states to grant universal suffrage. On

Thaddeus Stevens, address to the United States House of Representatives, Washington, DC, May 8, 1866.

June 13, 1866, Congress approved the amendment, which made freed slaves American citizens and guaranteed them equal protection under the laws.

U pon a careful survey of the whole ground, we did not believe that nineteen of the loyal States could be induced to ratify any proposition more stringent than [the Fourteenth Amendment]. I say nineteen, for I utterly repudiate and scorn the idea that any State not acting in the Union is to be counted on the question of ratification. . . .

Puerile Criticism

After having received the careful examination and approbation of the [Joint Committee on Reconstruction], and having received the united Republican vote of one hundred and twenty Representatives of the people, it was denounced as "utterly reprehensible," and "unpardonable"; "to be encountered as a public enemy"; "positively endangering the peace of the country, and covering its name with dishonor." "A wickedness on a larger scale than the crime against Kansas or the Fugitive Slave law; gross, foul, outrageous; an incredible injustice against the whole African race"; with every other vulgar epithet which polished cultivation could command. It was slaughtered by a puerile and pedantic criticism, by a perversion of philological definition which, if when I taught school a lad who had studied Lindley Murray had assumed, I would have expelled him from the institution as unfit to waste education upon. But it is dead, and unless this (less efficient, I admit) shall pass, its death has postponed the protection of the colored race perhaps for ages. But men in pursuit of justice must never despair. Let us again try and see whether we cannot devise some way to overcome the united forces of self-righteous Republicans and unrighteous copperheads [northerners who sympathized with the South]. It will not do for those who for thirty years have fought the beasts at Ephesus to be frightened by the fangs of modern catamounts.[1]

1. Ephesus was an ancient Greek city; catamount is another word for mountain lion.

An Excerpt from the Fourteenth Amendment

Section I. All persons born or naturalized in the United States, and subject to the jurisdiction thereof, are citizens of the United States and of the State wherein they reside. No State shall make or enforce any law which shall abridge the privileges or immunities of citizens of the United States; nor shall any State deprive any person of life, liberty, or property, without due process of law; nor deny to any person within its jurisdiction the equal protection of the laws.

The Fourteenth Amendment from the U.S. Constitution.

Let us now refer to the provisions of the proposed amendment. . . .

I can hardly believe that any person can be found who will not admit that every one of these provisions is just. They are all asserted, in some form or other, in our Declaration or organic law. But the Constitution limits only the action of Congress, and is not a limitation on the States. This amendment supplies that defect, and allows Congress to correct the unjust legislation of the States, so far that the law which operates upon one man shall operate *equally* upon all. Whatever law punishes a white man for a crime shall punish the black man precisely in the same way and to the same degree. Whatever law protects the white man shall afford "equal" protection to the black man. These are great advantages over their present codes. Now different degrees of punishment are inflicted, not on account of the magnitude of the crime, but according to the color of the skin. Now color disqualifies a man from testifying in courts, or being tried in the same way as white men. Unless the Constitution should restrain them those States will all, I fear, keep up this discrimination, and crush to death the hated freedmen. Some answer: "Your Civil Rights bill secures the same things." That is partly true, but a law is repealable by a majority. And I need hardly say that the first time that the South with their copperhead allies obtain the command of Congress it will be repealed. The veto of the President and their votes on the bill are conclusive evidence of that. This amendment once adopted cannot be annulled without two-thirds of Congress. That the enemies of the amendment will hardly get. And yet certain of our distinguished friends propose to admit State after State before this becomes a part of the Constitution. What madness! Is their judgment misled by their kindness; or are they unconsciously drifting into the haven of power at the other end of the avenue? I do not suspect it, but others will.

The second section I consider the most important in the article. The effect of this provision will be either to compel the States to grant universal suffrage or so to shear them of their power as to keep them forever in a hopeless minority in the national Government, both legislative and executive. If they do not enfranchise the freedmen, it would give to the rebel States but thirty-seven Representatives. Thus shorn of their power, they would soon become restive. Southern pride would not long brook a hopeless minority. True, it will take two, three, possibly five years before they conquer their prejudices sufficiently to allow their late slaves to become their equals at the polls. That short delay would not be injurious. In the meantime the freedmen would become more enlightened, and more fit to discharge the high duties of their new condition. In that time, too, the loyal Congress could mature their laws and so amend the Constitution as to secure the rights of every human being, and render disunion impossible. Heaven forbid that the Southern States, or *any of them*, should be represented on this floor until such muniments of freedom are built high and firm. Against our will they have been absent for four bloody years; against our will they must not come back until we are ready to receive them. Do not tell me that there are loyal Representatives waiting for admission—until their States are loyal they can have no standing here. They would merely *mis*represent their continents.

Punishing the Traitors

I admit that this article is not as good as the one we sent to death in the Senate. In my judgment we shall not approach the measure of justice until we have given every adult freedman a homestead on the land where he was born and toiled and suffered. Forty acres of land and a hut would be more valuable to him than the immediate right to vote. Unless we give them this we shall receive the censure of mankind and the curse of Heaven. That article referred to provided that if *one* of the injured race was excluded the State should forfeit the right to have any of them represented. That would have hastened their full enfranchisement. This section allows the States to discriminate among the same class, and receive proportionate credit in representation. This I dislike. But it is a short step forward. The large stride which we in vain proposed is dead; the murderers must answer to the suffering race. I would not have been the perpetrator. A load of misery must sit heavy on their souls.

The third section may encounter more difference of opinion here. Among the people I believe it will be the most popular of all the provisions; it prohibits rebels from voting for members of Congress and electors of President until 1870. My only objection to it is that it is too lenient. I know that there is a morbid sensibility, sometimes called mercy, which affects a few of all classes, from the priest to the clown, which has more sympathy for the murderer on the gallows than for his victim. I hope I have a heart as capable of feeling for human woe as others. I have long since wished that capital punishment were abolished. But I never dreamed that all punishment could be dispensed with in human society. Anarchy, *treason*, and violence would reign triumphant. Here is the mildest all punishments ever inflicted on traitors I might not consent to the extreme severity denounced upon them by a provincial governor of Tennessee—I mean the late lamented Andrew Johnson of blessed memory—but I would have increased the severity of this section. I would be glad to see it extended to 1876, and to include all State and municipal as well a national elections. In my judgment we do not sufficiently protect the loyal men of the Rebel States from the vindictive persecutions of their victorious Rebel neighbors. Still I will move no amendment, nor vote for any, lest the whole fabric should tumble to pieces.

I need say nothing of the fourth section, for none dare object to it who is not himself a rebel. To the friend of justice, the friend of the Union, of the perpetuity of liberty, and the final triumph of the rights of man and their extension to every human being, let me say, sacrifice as we have done your peculiar views, and, instead of vainly insisting upon the instantaneous operation of all that is right, accept what is possible, and "all these things shall be added unto you."

Viewpoint 2

"[The Fourteenth Amendment] is but another attempt . . . to consolidate in the Federal Government, by the action of Congress, all the powers claimed by the Czar of Russia."

The Fourteenth Amendment Should Not Be Supported

Andrew J. Rogers

Radical Republicans believed that a constitutional amendment was needed in order to guarantee citizenship and equality to former slaves. In response to these concerns, the Joint Committee on Reconstruction—a fifteen-member committee established by Congress in December 1865 to study conditions in the South and offer suggestions for reconstruction bills—began to draft the Fourteenth Amendment in 1866. Not surprisingly, many Democrats opposed the latest step in Radical Reconstruction. New Jersey Democrat Andrew J. Rogers—a minority member of the Joint Committee—states his opposition to the amendment in the following viewpoint. In his speech before Congress, Rogers argues that the U.S. Constitution does not allow the federal government to rule on the validity of state laws. He also asserts that state governments have the right to ban in-

Andrew J. Rogers, address before the United States Congress, Washington, DC, February 26, 1866.

terracial marriages, segregate schools, and pass other discriminatory laws. Despite Rogers's protestations, the amendment was passed by Congress on June 13, 1866.

No resolution proposing an amendment to the Constitution of the United States had been offered to this Congress more dangerous to the liberties of the people and the foundations of this Government than the pending resolution [Fourteenth Amendment]. When sifted from top to bottom it will be found to be the embodiment of centralization and the disfranchisement of the States of those sacred and immutable State rights which were reserved to them by the consent of our fathers in our organic law.

An Unnecessary Amendment

When the gentleman [Ohio representative John A. Bingham] says the proposed amendment is intended to authorize no rights except those already embodied in the Constitution, I give him the plain and emphatic answer—if the Constitution provides the requirements contained in this amendment, why, in this time of excitement and public clamor, should we attempt to again ingraft upon it what is already in it?. . .

The gentleman takes the position that there is nothing in this proposed amendment with regard to privileges and immunities of citizens of the several States attempted to be ingrafted in the instrument, except those which already exist in it. If those rights already exist in the organic law of the land, I ask him, what is the necessity of so amending the Constitution as to authorize Congress to carry into effect a plain provision which now, according to his views, inheres in the very organic law itself?

I know what the gentleman will attempt to say in answer to that position: that because the Constitution authorizes Congress to carry the powers conferred by it into effect, privileges and immunities are not considered within the meaning of powers, and therefore Congress has no right to carry into effect what the Constitution itself intended when it provided that citizens of each State should have all privileges and immunities of citizens in the several States.

Now, sir, the answer to that argument is simply this: that when the Constitution was framed and ratified, its makers did not intend to lodge in the Congress of the United States any power to override a State and settle by congressional legislation the rights, privileges, and immunities of citizens in the several States. That matter was left entirely for the courts, to enforce the privileges and immunities of the citizens under that clause of the organic law. Although our forefathers, in their wisdom, after having exacted and wrested from Great Britain State rights, saw fit to incorporate in the Constitution such a principle in regard to citizens of the several States, yet they never intended to give to Congress the power, by virtue of that clause, to control the local domain of a State or the privileges and immunities of citizens in the State, even though they had come from another State. . . .

But this proposed amendment goes much further than the Constitution goes in the language which it uses with regard to the privileges and immunities of citizens in the several States. It proposes so to amend it that all persons in the several States shall by act of Congress have equal protection in regard to life, liberty, and property. If the bill to protect all persons in the United States in their civil rights and furnish the means of their vindication, which has just passed the Senate by almost the entire vote of the Republican party be constitutional, what, I ask, is the use of this proposed amendment? What is the use of authorizing Congress to do more than Congress has already done, so far as one branch is concerned, in passing a bill to guaranty civil rights and immunities to the people of the United States without distinction of race or color? If it is necessary now to amend the Constitution of the United States in the manner in which the learned gentleman [Bingham] who reported this amendment proclaims, then the vote of the Senate of the United States in passing that bill guarantying civil rights to all without regard to race or color was an attempt to project legislation that was manifestly unconstitutional, and which this proposed amendment is to make legal. . . .

Rights Should Be Limited

My only hope for liberty is in the full restoration of all the States, with the rights of representation in the Congress of the United

States upon no condition but to take the oath laid down in the Constitution. In the legislation by the States they should look to the protection, security, advancement, and improvement, physically and intellectually, of all classes, as well the blacks as the whites. Negroes should have the channels of education opened to them by the States, and by the States they should be protected in life, liberty, and property, and by the States should be allowed all the rights of being witnesses, of suing and being sued, of contracting, and doing every act or thing that a white man is authorized by law to do. But to give to them the right of suffrage, and hold office, and marry whites, in my judgment is dangerous and never ought to be extended to them by any State. However, that is a matter belonging solely to the sovereign will of the States. I have faith in the people, and dark and gloomy as the hour is, I do not despair of free government. I plant myself upon the will of God to work out a bright destiny for the American people. . . .

Who gave the Senate the constitutional power to pass that bill guarantying equal rights to all, if it is necessary to amend the organic law in the manner proposed by this joint resolution? This is but another attempt to consolidate the power of the States in the Federal Government. It is another step to an imperial despotism. It is but another attempt to blot out from that flag the eleven stars that represent the States of the South and to consolidate in the Federal Government, by the action of Congress, all the powers claimed by the Czar of Russia or the Emperor of the French. It provides that all persons in the several States shall have equal protection in the right of life, liberty, and property. Now, it is claimed by gentlemen upon the other side of the House [Republicans] that negroes are citizens of the United States. Suppose that in the State of New Jersey negroes are citizens, as they are claimed to be by the other side of the House, and they change their residence to the State of South Carolina, if this amendment be passed Congress can pass under it a law compelling South Carolina to grant to negroes every right accorded to white people there; and as white men there have the right to marry white women, negroes, under this amendment, would be entitled to the same right; and thus miscegenation and mixture of the races could be authorized in any State, as all citizens under this amendment are entitled to the same privileges and immunities, and the same protection in life, liberty, and property. . . .

The organic law says that no person but a natural-born citizen, or a citizen when it was made, shall be eligible to the office of President. This amendment would make all citizens eligible, negroes as well as whites. For if negroes are citizens, they are natural born, because they are the descendants of ancestors for several generations back, who were born here as well as themselves. The negroes cannot be citizens in a new State in which they may take up their residence unless they are entitled to the privileges and immunities of the citizens resident in that State. Most of the States make a distinction in the rights of married women. This would authorize Congress to repeal all such distinctions.

Marriage is a contract as set down in all the books from the Year-books down to the present time. A white citizen of any State may marry a white woman; but if a black citizen goes into the same State he is entitled to the same privileges and immunities that white citizens have, and therefore under this amendment a negro might be allowed to marry a white woman. I will not go for an amendment of the Constitution to give a power so dangerous, so likely to degrade the white men and women of this country, which would put it in the power of fanaticism in times of excitement and civil war to allow the people of any State to mingle and mix themselves by marriage with negroes so as to run the pure white blood of the Anglo-Saxon people of the country into the black blood of the negro or the copper blood of the Indian.

Taking Away the Power of the States

Now, sir, the words "privileges and immunities" in the Constitution of the United States have been construed by the courts of the several States to mean privileges and immunities in a limited extent. . . . Those words, as now contained in the Constitution of the United States, were used in a qualified sense, and subject to the local control, dominion, and the sovereignty of the States. But this act of Congress proposes to amend the Constitution so as to take away the rights of the States with regard to the life, liberty, and property of the people, so as to enable and empower Congress to pass laws compelling the abrogation of all the statutes of the States which make a distinction, for instance, between a crime committed by a white man and a crime committed by a black man, or allow white people privileges, immunities, or property not allowed to a black man.

Take the State of Kentucky, for instance. According to her laws, if a negro commits a rape upon a white woman he is punished by death. If a white man commits that offense, the punishment is imprisonment. Now, according to this proposed amendment, the Congress of the United States is to have the right to repeal the law of Kentucky and compel that State to inflict the same punishment upon a white man for rape as upon a black man.

According to the organic law of Indiana a negro is forbidden to come there and hold property. This amendment would abrogate and blot out forever that law, which is valuable in the estimation of the sovereign people of Indiana.

In the State of Pennsylvania there are laws which make a distinction with regard to the schooling of white children and the schooling of black children. It is provided that certain schools shall be designated and set apart for white children, and certain other schools designated and set apart for black children. Under this amendment, Congress would have power to compel the State to provide for white children and black children to attend the same school, upon the principle that all the people in the several States shall have equal protection in all the rights of life, liberty, and property, and all the privileges and immunities of citizens in the several States.

The effect of this proposed amendment is to take away the power of the States; to interfere with the internal police and regulations of the States; to centralize a consolidated power in this Federal Government which our fathers never intended should be exercised by it.

Viewpoint 3

"Most [carpetbaggers] have titles, not empty titles complaisantly bestowed in piping times of peace, but titles worthily won by faithful and efficient service in the Federal armies."

Carpetbaggers Have Helped the South

Alexander White

Carpetbagger was the epithet that many southerners used to describe the northerners who had relocated to the former rebel territories after the Civil War, men whom they believed had moved to the South for personal gain and political opportunities. The word was derived from the idea that these northerners had placed all of their possessions in a carpetbag for the journey south. Many southerners particularly disliked carpetbaggers because most of these migrants were Radical Republicans.

However, some southerners, known derisively as scalawags for their support of Republicans and their reconstruction plans, sympathized with the carpetbaggers. One such man was Alexander White, a Republican representative from Alabama. In a statement before the House of Representatives in February 1875, White argues that both the North and the South have wrongly maligned the carpetbaggers. He states that most of these men were valiant soldiers who did not move to the South for political reasons but merely stayed after the war was over to

Alexander White, address to the United States House of Representatives, Washington, DC, February 1875.

grow cotton. White also contends that the nation fears carpet-baggers and scalawags because those two groups have helped ensure that black Republicans will succeed in politics.

White republicans are known by the contemptuous appellation of carpet-bagger and scalawag, names conferred upon them by the chivalry, in whose political interest prowl the bands of Ku-Klux and White League assassins in the South, and as such, especially the carpet-bagger, they have become a by-word and reproach. We of the South are not responsible for them; they are a northern growth, and unless going South expatriates them, they are still northern men, even as you are—bone of your bone, flesh of your flesh. But who are they? I can speak for my State, for I think I know nearly all in the State, and there are a good many of them. Most of them have titles, not empty titles complaisantly bestowed in piping times of peace, but titles worthily won by faithful and efficient service in the Federal armies, or plucked with strong right arm from war's rugged front upon the field of battle. Many of them bear upon their bodies scars of wounds received while fighting under your flag for the nation's life and the country's glory. These men either went South with the Union armies and at the close of the war remained there, or went there soon after, in the latter part of 1865 or early in 1866, to make cotton. The high price of cotton in 1865 and 1866, and the facility with which cheap labor could be obtained, induced many enterprising northern men, especially the officers in the Federal armies in the South who had seen and become familiar with the country, to go or remain there to make cotton. Many purchased large plantations and paid large sums of money for them; others rented plantations, in some instances two or three, and embarked with characteristic energy in planting. This, it should be remembered, was before the civil-rights bill or the reconstruction acts, before the colored people had any part in political matters, and two years before they ever proposed to vote or claimed to have the right to vote at any election in the Southern States.

When the political contests of 1868 came on in which the colored people first took a part in politics, as near all the native population in the large cotton-growing sections were opposed to negro suffrage and opposed to the republican party, they very naturally turned to these northern men for counsel and assistance in the performance of the new duties and exercise of their newly acquired political rights, and they as naturally gave them such counsel and became their leaders, and were intrusted with official power by them.

This brief summary will give you a correct idea of the manner in which, as I believe, nine-tenths of those who are called carpetbaggers became involved in political affairs [in the] South, and dispose of a very large part of the slanders which have been promulgated against them not only by their political enemies at the South, but by the treacherous northern knaves who, under the pretense of being republicans and as correspondents of so-called republican papers at the North, have gone down South prepared in advance to stab the cause of justice and of truth, of humanity and freedom, of the law and the Constitution, to the heart. Could these miserable miscreants have known with what ineffable contempt they were regarded by the very men whose credulous dupes they were, with what scathing scorn they regarded northern men who would lend themselves to traduce whole classes of northern men, who would allow themselves to be used as the tools to break down the political party to which they professed to belong, it would have diminished much the self-complacency with which their work was done. They could have realized that southern men, though bold and often reckless of the means by which they seek to attain political ends, that earnest and vehement, ardent and high-spirited, under the influence of one great ultimate aim to which all else is subordinated, they may reach politically to the parallel of the dogma which once prevailed in the religious world, "there is no faith to be kept with heretics," yet they can never be brought to descend to sympathy with or respect for such low-browed infamy as theirs.

These two classes, the carpet-baggers and scalawag[s], are the object of peculiar assault by the democracy, for they know that these constitute the bulwark of the republican party in the South. Without their co-operation and assistance the colored republicans could neither organize nor operate successfully in political contests, and without them the party would soon be extinguished in the Southern States.

Viewpoint 4

"A carpet-bagger is generally understood to be a man . . . of an ignorant or bad character, and who seeks to array the negroes against the whites."

Carpetbaggers Have Harmed the South

William Manning Lowe

Carpetbagger was the epithet used to describe northerners who had relocated to the South after the Civil War; the name implied that these northerners had placed all of their possessions in a carpetbag and moved to the South for personal gain, such as obtaining public office. These northerners—most of whom were Radical Republicans eager to impart their views on the southern populace—enjoyed considerable political opportunities; the Fourteenth Amendment and the Reconstruction Acts of 1867 had restricted ex-Confederates, who were almost exclusively southern Democrats, from voting and holding political office.

On October 13, 1871, members of the Joint Select Committee to Inquire into the Condition of Affairs in the Late Insurrectionary States, questioned Alabama lawyer and former Confederate colonel William Manning Lowe about the South's opinion of carpetbaggers. In his testimony, excerpted in the following viewpoint, Lowe maintains that carpetbaggers gained office by inciting freed slaves against white southerners, leading to unrest throughout the South.

William Manning Lowe, testimony before the Joint Select Committee to Inquire into the Condition of Affairs in the Late Insurrectionary States, Washington, DC, October 13, 1871.

I regard the most aggravating and disagreeable fact in the whole business of reconstruction to have been the intrusion of what is known in the South as the carpet-bag element. General [George] Spencer and General [Willard] Warner were elected to the Senate of the United States, . . . both of them men recently coming into the State, and men whom we supposed and whom we considered as the representatives of the negro race, in combined hostility to the white race. . . .

Question. Were the county officers of the same stripe?

Answer. I believe so, sir; they were in a great degree of the same character. . . . The carpet-bag element took the lead in the formation of the [new state] constitution, and in holding all the offices, and in carrying the State back in the reconstruction policy, and I regard that as the prolific source of a great deal of trouble and prejudice and bitterness. . . .

Question. Is there any prejudice at all in this State against northern men who came here for the purpose of carrying on business, and following any avocation, and to mingle their fortunes with those of the people of this State as citizens?

Answer. No, sir; on the contrary, there is a very earnest desire that they shall come. . . .

Defining the Term

Question. You have used the epithets "carpet-baggers," and "scalawags," repeatedly, during the course of your testimony. I wish you would give us an accurate definition of what a carpet-bagger is and what a scalawag is.

Answer. Well, sir, the term carpet-bagger is not applied to northern men who come here to settle in the South, but a carpet-bagger is generally understood to be a man who comes here for office sake, of an ignorant or bad character, and who seeks to array the negroes against the whites; who is a kind of political dry-nurse for the negro population, in order to get office through them.

Question. Then it does not necessarily suppose that he should be a northern man?

Answer. Yes, sir; it does suppose that he is to be a northern man, but it does not apply to all northern men that come here.

Question. If he is an intelligent, educated man, and comes here for office, then he is not a carpet-bagger, I understand?

Answer. No, sir; we do not generally call them carpet-baggers.

Question. If he is a northern man possessed of good character and seeks office he is not a carpet-bagger?

Answer. Mr. Chairman, there are so few northern men who come here of intelligence and character, that join the republican party and look for office alone to the negroes, that we have never made a class for them. I have never heard them classified. . . . But the term "carpet-bagger" was applied to the office-seeker from the North who comes here seeking office by the negroes, by arraying their political passions and prejudices against the white people of the community.

Question. The man in addition to that, under your definition, must be an ignorant man and of bad character?

Answer. Yes, sir; he is generally of that description. We regard any man as a man of bad character who seeks to create hostility between the races.

Question. Do you regard any republican as a bad character who seeks to obtain the suffrages of the negro population?

Answer. We regard any republican or any man as a man of bad character, whether he is native or foreign born, who seeks to obtain office from the negroes by exciting their passions and prejudices against the whites. We think that a very great evil—very great. We are very intimately associated with the negro race; we have a large number in the country, and we think it essential that we shall live in peace together.

Two Southern Senators

Question. Do you regard Senators Warner and Spencer as in the category of carpet-baggers?

Answer. Yes, sir. . . .

Question. Do you regard Senator Spencer as an ignorant man and of bad character?

Answer. I have a very slight acquaintance with General Spencer; I know him; I do not think him an ignorant man; I think him, with the authority of those who know him intimately and well, to be an unprincipled man. Ex-Governor William H. Smith, of this State, in the last campaign, published a letter . . . containing a statement to the effect that Senator Spencer lived upon the pas-

This illustration depicts carpetbaggers as many southerners regarded them: greedy, white northerners seeking personal gain and political influence.

sions and prejudices of the races; that the breath of peace would leave him on the surface, neglected and despised.

Question. I am not asking for Governor Smith's opinion, but your own?

Answer. Well, sir, I believe Governor Smith.

Question. Did Senator Spencer seek to array the negroes against the whites?

Answer. Yes, sir. One of his shysters and agents here, in the last election when I was a candidate, circulated the most infamous lies about me all over the county, to the effect that I would deprive the colored people of the substance of personal freedom if I got into office, although I told them the contrary; that I would deprive them of suffrage if I got into office; that I would do everything to injure them in person and property. His agents who were in his confidence did this. They told me they were in his confidence, and I have no doubt they did it to subserve his political interests. . . .

Southern Accomplices

Question. Having given a definition of the carpet-bagger, you may now define scalawag.

Answer. A scalawag is his subservient tool and accomplice, who is a native of the country.

Question. How many of the white race in the county of Madison vote the republican ticket?

Answer. I do not think, and I have very accurate means of judging, that a hundred ever voted it.

Question. You class them all as carpet-baggers and scalawags?

Answer. Yes, sir.

Question. Are all of them seeking office?

Answer. No, sir.

Question. Are all of them ignorant men and of bad character?

Answer. No, sir.

Question. Are all of them natives of the Northern States?

Answer. No, sir.

Question. Why do you classify them as carpet-baggers and scalawags?

Answer. I have told you that I classified as carpet-baggers those who came down here, who come within that definition, coming down here and seeking office from the negroes by arraying their passions and prejudices against the white people. I classed the others as scalawags. They are more or less scalawaggers, according to the part they play in this political programme.

Question. What proportion of this one hundred white men who vote the republican ticket are seeking office?

Answer. It would be impossible for me to say. I believe that there are very few of them that would decline to serve their country in a lucrative office if they could get it. . . .

Question. How do you classify Captain [Lionel W.] Day, who is clerk, I believe, of the district court of the United States, and *ex officio* commissioner?

Answer. He has never been politically classed. He never took any part in politics at all.

Question. Does he hold office under the Federal Government?
Answer. Yes, sir.
Question. Do you regard him as a carpet-bagger?
Answer. No, sir.
Question. A northern man?
Answer. Yes, sir.
Question. Did he come here seeking office?
Answer. No, sir.
Question. Did he come into the State seeking an office?
Answer. No, sir; I do not think he did. I do not know that he did.
Question. Has he not held office in some capacity all through since he came?
Answer. I do not know. I never knew him until he came here.
Question. What distinguishes him from the genuine carpet-bagger?
Answer. Because he does not associate with the negroes; he does not seek their society, politically or socially; he has nothing to do with them any more than any other white gentleman in the community.
Question. He votes with the democratic party?. . .
Answer. I think he did.
Question. Was he not a democratic delegate to [the state constitutional] convention?
Answer. Yes, sir; he was spoken of as a candidate himself, but he did not desire the nomination. He told me he did not want it. He said he did not think it was reputable for a northern man to come down here and be seeking offices that southern men could hold, and he preferred his name should not be mentioned.
Question. As I want to get at the true definition of these terms, I will inquire of you if a northern man comes into Alabama intent upon obtaining office, and seeks to obtain an office through the instrumentality of the democratic organization, is he a carpet-bagger?
Answer. No, sir; the term is never applied to a democrat under any circumstances. . . . No democrat who seeks office through the virtue, intelligence, and property of the country, who says, "Gentleman, your best men are disfranchised by the act of Congress; I do not care particularly about office, but as you cannot hold it I will go there, knock your chains off, and get you a chance."

Viewpoint 5

"The organization was simply . . . a brotherhood of the property-holders, the peaceable, law-abiding citizens of the State, for self-protection."

The Ku Klux Klan Is a Peacekeeping Organization

John Brown Gordon

White southern Democrats founded the Ku Klux Klan in the aftermath of the Civil War. The organization's efforts to return the South to its prewar status were marked by violence against white Republicans and southern blacks. In 1871, after hearing reports of whippings and lynchings, the U.S. Congress established the Joint Select Committee to Inquire into the Condition of Affairs in the Late Insurrectionary States in order to investigate the Klan and other secret organizations.

John Brown Gordon, an Atlanta lawyer and former lieutenant general in the Confederate army, was one of the men questioned by the committee. Although he did not name the organization to which he belonged, Gordon was a prominent member of the Georgia Klan. In his testimony, excerpted below, Gordon contends that these secret organizations were founded in response to the growing membership of blacks in the Union

John Brown Gordon, testimony before the Joint Select Committee to Inquire into the Condition of Affairs in the Late Insurrectionary States, Washington, DC, 1872.

League, a political group founded by northern Republicans during the period immediately following the war when most white southerners were barred from voting or holding political office. He also claims that these societies were necessary in order to keep the peace and guard against attacks by recently freed slaves.

Q*uestion.* What do you know of any combinations in Georgia, known as Ku-Klux, or by any other name, who have been violating the law?

Answer. I do not know anything about any Ku-Klux organization, as the papers talk about it. I have never heard of anything of that sort except in the papers and by general report; but I do know that an organization did exist in Georgia at one time. I know that in 1868—I think that was the time—I was approached and asked to attach myself to a secret organization in Georgia. I was approached by some of the very best citizens of the State—some of the most peaceable, law-abiding men, men of large property, who had large interests in the State. The object of this organization was explained to me at the time by these parties; and I want to say that I approved of it most heartily. I would approve again of a similar organization, under the same state of circumstances.

Question. Tell us about what that organization was.

Answer. The organization was simply this—nothing more and nothing less: it was an organization, a brotherhood of the property-holders, the peaceable, law-abiding citizens of the State, for self-protection. The instinct of self-protection prompted that organization; the sense of insecurity and danger, particularly in those neighborhoods where the negro population largely predominated. The reasons which led to this organization were three or four. The first and main reason was the organization of the Union League, as they called it, about which we knew nothing more than this: that the negroes would desert the plantations, and go off at night in large numbers; and on being asked where they had been, would reply, sometimes, "We have been to the muster;" sometimes, "We have been to the lodge;" sometimes, "We have been to the meeting." Those things were observed for a great length of time. We knew that the "carpet-baggers," as the people of Georgia called these men who came from a distance and had no interest at all with us; who were unknown to us entirely; who from all we could learn about them did not have any very exalted position at their homes—these men were organizing the colored people. We knew that beyond all question. We knew of certain instances where great crimes had been committed; where overseers had been driven from plantations, and the negroes had asserted their right to hold the property for their own benefit. Apprehension took possession of the entire public mind of the State. Men were in many instances afraid to go away from their homes and leave their wives and children, for fear of outrage. Rapes were already being committed in the country. There was this general organization of the black race on the one hand, and an entire disorganization of the white race on the other hand. We were afraid to have a public organization; because we supposed it would be construed at once, by the authorities at Washington, as an organization antagonistic to the Government of the United States. It was therefore necessary, in order to protect our families from outrage and preserve our own lives, to have something that we could regard as a brotherhood— a combination of the best men of the country, to act purely in self-defense, to repel the attack in case we should be attacked by these people. That was the whole object of this organization. I never heard of any disguises connected with it; we had none, very certainly. This organization, I think, extended nearly all over the State. It was, as I say, an organization purely for self-defense. It had no more politics in it than the organization of the Masons. I never heard the idea of politics suggested in connection with it.

A Peace Police Organization

Question. Did it have any antagonism toward either the State or the Federal Government?

Answer. None on earth—not a particle. On the contrary, it was purely a peace police organization, and I do know of some instances where it did prevent bloodshed on a large scale. I know of one case in Albany, Georgia, where, but for the instrumentality of this organization, there would have been, beyond all doubt, a conflict, growing out of a personal difficulty between a black man and

a white man. The two races gathered on each side, but this organization quelled the trouble easily and restored peace, without any
violence to anybody, and without a particle of difficulty with either the black race or the white. They stopped one just as much as
they did the other. This society was purely a police organization
to keep the peace, to prevent disturbances in our State. That was
the motive that actuated me in going into it, and that was the
whole object of the organization, as explained to me by these persons who approached me. I approved of the object.

Question. You had no riding about at nights?

Answer. None on earth. I have no doubt that such things have
occurred in Georgia. It is notoriously stated—I have no personal
knowledge of anything of the kind, but I have reason to believe
it—that disguised parties have committed outrages in Georgia;
but we have discovered in some cases that these disguised parties
did not belong to any particular party. We have demonstrated that
beyond all question in some cases, by bringing to trial and conviction parties who belonged, for instance, to the radical [repub-
lican] party, who had in disguise committed outrages in the State.
There is not a good man in Georgia who does not deplore that
thing just as much as any radical deplores it. When I use the term
"radical," I do not mean to reflect upon the republican party generally; but in our State a republican is a very different sort of a man
from a republican generally in the Northern States. In our State
republicanism means nothing in the world but creating distur-
bance, riot, and animosity, and filching and plundering. That is
what it means in our State—nothing else; there is no politics in it.
In the North the thing is very different. There men can differ in
politics, and yet have the kindliest relations; in Georgia we cannot
do it unless we are willing to countenance all sorts of outrages
upon our people. There are genteel republicans in Georgia, who
are just as safe as any one else; who travel all over the State; who
occupy high positions, and are never insulted in the street, the
cars, or anywhere else. If there is any organization in Georgia for
the purpose of putting down republicanism there, why does it not
attack the leaders of that party? It strikes me as the very highest
commentary upon the law-abiding spirit of the people of Georgia
that such men as I could name—men in high position who have

plundered our people by the million—still live and are countenanced on the streets, have no insults offered to them. The truth is simply this: that individuals in Georgia of all parties and all colors have, I suppose, committed outrage; but such affairs have been purely personal, just as they are when they occur anywhere else in the United States. I do not believe any more crimes have been committed in Georgia than in any other community of the same number anywhere else in the country. That is my honest conviction. I do not believe that any crime has ever been committed by this organization of which I have spoken, and of which I was a member. I believe it was purely a peace police—a law-abiding concern. That was its whole object, and it never would have existed but for the apprehension in the minds of our people of a conflict in which we would have had no sympathy and no protection. We apprehended that the sympathy of the entire Government would be against us; and nothing in the world but the instinct of self-protection prompted that organization. We felt that we must at any cost protect ourselves, our homes, our wives and children from outrage. We would have preferred death rather than to have submitted to what we supposed was coming upon us. At this time I do not believe any such organization exists, or has existed for a long time. I have not heard of it for two years, I am certain.

Dissolving the Organization

Question. Why did it cease to exist; why did it pass away?

Answer. Well, sir, it just dissolved because the courts became generally established; and though the courts were in the hands of the opposite party, our people believed they were trying to do justice; that a general protection was extended over us. Our people thought we could get justice at the hands of these judges; though they were of the opposite party, and though negroes were on the juries, we were satisfied that in the existing condition of things we were safe. Since Governor [Rufus] Bullock's election [in 1868] I have not heard anything of that organization. I am not sure that it did not pass away with his election. It certainly has not existed since within my knowledge; and I think I would have known it if it had. I think that my position would have brought it to my knowledge if any such organization had existed for several years past. As I have stated, the only reason it has passed away is, I think, because the people felt safe. Courts were established and police regulations were generally instituted.

You must remember that we were in a state of anarchy there for a long time. We had no law but drum-head courts-martial. Our people were entirely powerless to do anything. We always felt that if the Federal troops were kept in our midst we would be protected. I want to state that with great emphasis. Our people have always felt that if the white troops of the Federal Army could have been stationed in our midst in those negro belts we would have been safe. But the troops were perhaps two hundred miles away; and before they could have been brought to our relief the whole neighborhood might have been slaughtered. We then believed that such a thing might occur on almost any night. Such was the condition of things in Georgia at that time. I do not believe that it exists now, or has existed for two years. To my certain knowledge this organization never did exist as a political organization. I do not know what may have been the case elsewhere; but very certainly there was no politics in this thing in Georgia, so far as I had anything to do with it; and I think that the organization was of the same character all over the State—probably over the South wherever it existed. We never called it Ku-Klux, and therefore I do not know anything about Ku-Klux.

Viewpoint 6

"Because [Dr. Winsmith] has dared become a Republican, . . . he has become the doomed victim of the murderous Ku Klux Klan."

The Ku Klux Klan Is a Terrorist Organization

Joseph H. Rainey

Radical Republicans faced opposition both inside and outside of their party. The most dangerous of these opponents were the members of the Ku Klux Klan. The Klan was formed after the Civil War by white Southern Democrats who sought to regain control of the war-torn region, which was governed during Reconstruction by Radical Republican politicians. Klan members held secret meetings where they planned violent acts, including murder, against blacks and their Radical Republican advocates. In the following viewpoint, excerpted from his statement before Congress, South Carolina representative Joseph H. Rainey details some of the Klan's atrocities and charges that the nation must pass laws that will protect the life and liberty of black Southerners and white Republicans. Rainey, a Republican, was the nation's first black congressman.

Joseph H. Rainey, testimony before the Forty-Second Congress, First Session, April 1, 1871.

I need not, Mr. Speaker, recite here the murderous deeds committed both in North and South Carolina. I could touch the feelings of this House by the story of widows and orphans now wandering amid the ravines of the rural counties of my native State seeking protection and maintenance from others who are yet unable, on account of their own poverty, to grant them aid. I could dwell upon the sorrows of poor women, with their helpless infants, cast upon the world, homeless and destitute, deprived of their natural protectors by the red hand of the midnight assassin. I could appeal to you, members upon this floor, as husbands and fathers, to picture to yourselves the desolation of your own happy firesides should you be suddenly snatched away from your loved ones. Think of gray-haired men, whose fourscore years are almost numbered, the venerated heads of peaceful households, without warning murdered for political opinion's sake. In proof I send to the desk the following article and ask the Clerk to read. It is taken from the *Spartanburg (South Carolina) Republican*, March 29, 1871.

An Outrage in South Carolina

The Clerk read as follows:

"*Horrible Attempt at Murder by Disguised Men.*—One of the most cowardly and inhuman attempts at murder known in the annals of crime was made last Wednesday night, the 22d instant, by a band of disguised men upon the person of Dr. J. Winsmith at his home about twelve miles from town. The doctor, a man nearly seventy years of age, had been to town during the day and was seen and talked with by many of our citizens. Returning home late, he soon afterward retired, worn out and exhausted by the labors of the day. A little after midnight he was aroused by some one knocking violently at his front door. The knocking was soon afterward repeated at his chamber door, which opens immediately upon the front yard. The doctor arose, opened the door, and saw two men in disguise standing before him. As soon as he appeared one of the men cried out, 'Come on boys! Here's the damned old rascal.' The doctor immediately stepped back into the room, picked up two singlebarreled pistols lying upon the bureau, and returned to the open door. At his reappearance the men retreated behind some cedar trees standing in the yard. The doctor, in his night clothes, boldly stepped out into the yard and followed them. On reaching the trees he fired, but with what effect he does not know. He continued to advance, when twenty or thirty shots were fired at him by men crouched behind an orange hedge. He fired his remaining pistol and then attempted to return to the house. Before reaching it, however, he sank upon the ground exhausted by the loss of blood, and pain, occasioned by seven wounds which he had received in various parts of his body. As soon as he fell the assassins mounted their horses and rode away.

"The doctor was carried into the house upon a quilt, borne by his wife and some colored female servants. The colored men on the premises fled on the approach of the murderers, and the colored women being afraid to venture out, Mrs. Winsmith herself was obliged to walk three quarters of a mile to the house of her nephew, Dr. William Smith, for assistance. The physician has been with Dr. Winsmith day and night since the difficulty occurred, and thinks, we learn, that there is a possible chance of the doctor's recovery.

The Klan Lengthened Reconstruction

Historian Rembert W. Patrick, in the following passage from his book The Reconstruction of the Nation, *suggests that the Ku Klux Klan's efforts to defeat southern Republicans might have backfired. According to Patrick, the Klan's criminal acts served to lengthen, rather than stymie, congressional reconstruction.*

Even today it remains impossible to assess some effects of the Klan. Certainly it failed in 1868 to prevent the establishment of Republican governments. The reiterated claim that it destroyed the Loyal League [a group comprised primarily of blacks who sought to strengthen the Republican vote] has no foundation in fact. The league accomplished its avowed mission in making the Negro politically conscious and then shifted its activities to other fields. In reality the Negro had nothing to sustain him as a voter and officeholder. He neither possessed the property nor had the education to give him competitive

"The occasion of this terrible outrage can be only the fact that Dr. Winsmith is a Republican. One of the largest land-holders and tax-payers in the county, courteous in manner, kind in disposition, and upright and just in all his dealings with his fellowmen, he has ever been regarded as one of the leading citizens of the county. For many years prior to the war he represented the people in the Legislature, and immediately after the war he was sent to the senate. Because he has dared become a Republican, believing that in the doctrines of true republicanism only can the State and country find lasting peace and prosperity, he has become the doomed victim of the murderous Ku Klux Klan.

"The tragedy has cast a gloom over the entire community, and while we are glad to say that it has generally been condemned, yet we regret to state that no step has yet been taken to trace out and punish the perpetrators of the act. The judge of this circuit is sitting on his bench; the machinery of justice is in working order; but there can be found no hand bold enough to set it in motion.

---

status in the political arena. Without support from Northerners he was doomed to second-class citizenship.

Southerners believed that the Ku Klux Klan speeded the restoration of home rule in some southern states, but this opinion is open to question. The obvious criminality of the Klan incensed many Northerners who were growing tired of the "Southern Problem" and showing a willingness to "Let the South govern the South." President [Ulysses S.] Grant had no real concern for the Negro and his call for peace, for letting the South alone, was applauded by millions of northern voters. But the outrages perpetrated by the Klan aroused southern and northern Republicans to enact restrictive legislation. On the whole, instead of speeding the defeat of Republicans in the South, the Klan lengthened the period of Congressional Reconstruction.

Rembert W. Patrick, *The Reconstruction of the Nation*. London: Oxford University Press, 1967.

The courts of justice seem paralyzed when they have to meet such issues as this. Daily reports come to us of men throughout the country being whipped; of schoolhouses for colored children being closed, and of parties being driven from their houses and their families. Even here in town there are some who fear to sleep at their own homes and in their own beds. The law affords no protection for life and property in this county, and the sooner the country knows it and finds a remedy for it, the better it will be. Better a thousand times the rule of the bayonet than the humiliating lash of the Ku Klux and the murderous bullet of a midnight assassin.". . .

Protecting Union Supporters

It has been asserted that protection for the colored people only has been demanded; and in this there is a certain degree of truth, because they are noted for their steadfastness to the Union and the cause of liberty as guarantied by the Constitution. But, on the other hand, this protection is equally desired for those loyal whites, some to the manner born, others who, in the exercise of their natural rights as American citizens, have seen fit to remove thither from other sections of the States, and who are now undergoing persecution simply on account of their activity in carrying out Union principles and loyal sentiments in the South. Their efforts have contributed largely to further reconstruction and the restoration of the southern States to the old fellowship of the Federal compact. It is indeed hard that their reward for their well-meant earnestness should be that of being violently treated, and even forced to flee from the homes of their choice. It will be a foul stain upon the escutcheon of our land if such atrocities be tamely suffered longer to continue.

In the dawn of our freedom our young Republic was widely recognized and proudly proclaimed to the world the refuge, the safe asylum of the oppressed of all lands. Shall it be said that at this day, through mere indifference and culpable neglect, this grand boast of ours is become a mere form of words, an utter fraud? I earnestly hope not! And yet, if we stand with folded arms and idle hands, while the cries of our oppressed brethren sound in our ears, what will it be but a proof to all men that we are utterly unfit for our glorious mission, unworthy our noble privileges, as the greatest of republics, the champions of freedom for all men? I would that every individual man in this whole nation could be aroused to a sense of his own part and duty in this great question. When we call to mind the fact that this persecution is waged against men for the simple reason that they dare to vote with the party which has saved the Union intact by the lavish expenditure of blood and treasure, and has borne the nation safely through the fearful crisis of these last few years, our hearts swell with an overwhelming indignation. . . .

I say to the gentlemen of the Opposition, and to the entire membership of the Democratic party, that upon your hands rests the blood of the loyal men of the South. Disclaim it as you will the stain is there to prove your criminality before God and the world in the day of retribution which will surely come. I pity the man or party of men who would seek to ride into power over the dead body of a legitimate opponent.

Viewpoint 7

"Johnson's formula for peaceful reconciliation had merits."

Johnson's Reconstruction Plan Had Merit

Chester G. Hearn

President Andrew Johnson had a difficult presidency that is best known for his impeachment—which had been prompted by Johnson's attempts to remove Secretary of War Edwin Stanton without receiving congressional consent—and near-conviction by the U.S. Congress. Johnson is also infamous for his failure to implement a successful reconstruction program. Chester G. Hearn defends the president in the following viewpoint. According to Hearn, Johnson had a thoughtful plan to reconstruct the United States, which might have succeeded had it not been for the attitudes of the Radical Republicans who controlled Congress. Although Hearn acknowledges that Johnson made little effort to work with Congress, he contends that the president was right when he advocated states' rights and expressed distaste for the less forgiving approach of congressional reconstruction. Hearn is the author of many books on the Civil War and Reconstruction, including *The Impeachment of Andrew Johnson*, from which the following viewpoint has been excerpted.

Chester G. Hearn, *The Impeachment of Andrew Johnson*. Jefferson, NC: McFarland & Company, Inc., 2000. Copyright © 2000 by Chester G. Hearn. Reproduced by permission.

Johnson's departure from a life of politics left him with a legacy unlike any other president. Because he held office during the period of Reconstruction when Radicals ruled, his reputation alternately rose and fell depending upon the opinions of both advocates and detractors. No impeached president can escape criticism, regardless of the validity of the underlying reasons. Johnson's courageous protection of the Constitution cannot be challenged on its merits, but his obstinate methods can be questioned because compromise never came easy for Andrew Johnson.

Like his predecessor, Johnson was unfashionable among public men of the period because of his meticulous honesty. When a group from New York City offered him a fine carriage and a span of horses, he rejected the offer on the ground that he had always made it a practice to refuse gifts while in public station. When handling millions of dollars as military governor of Tennessee, he left office poorer than when he entered it—which many patriots of the time condemned as outright stupidity. The House Impeachment Committee spent two years investigating every transaction Johnson made and never found so much as a scrap on which to hang an allegation. Scarcely one among his traducers could have stood the same microscopic test without suffering political pain.

Among a number of capable historical scholars, one discovered that Johnson, when preparing speeches or veto messages, formed his "opinions on great questions of public policy as diligent as any man in seeking and weighing the views of all who were competent to aid him." The White House staff were amazed at his tireless energy. He kept six secretaries busy and "except for an hour or so in the afternoon and at meal times rarely left his desk until midnight." Henry Adams, an intellectual both admired and criticized for his snobbery, admitted when recalling his youthful prejudices of being "surprised to realize how strong the Executive was in 1868—perhaps the strongest he was ever to see."

When the Supreme Court overturned the Tenure of Office Act[1]

---

1. The Tenure of Office Act, passed by Congress on March 2, 1867, forbade the President from removing any federal officeholder who had been appointed by the consent of the Senate unless he received further approval from the Senate. Johnson's alleged violation of the act led to his impeachment. In 1926 the Supreme Court ruled that the act was unconstitutional.

in the 1920s, historians took another look at Andrew Johnson and revived his attributes. When civil rights issues erupted in the 1960s, scholars looked once more at Johnson's policies and blamed him for repressing racial solutions for one hundred years. The Radicals, however, overturned presidential vetoes on every important civil rights issue. Although many in the south heard Johnson's voice, he cannot be blamed for the corrupt carpetbaggers who, supported by Radical legislation, created the polarization between blacks and whites that continued through the twentieth century.

Battling the Radical Republicans

Johnson understood life in the south better than he understood life in the north. Radicals only understood life in the north. The day of the Jacksonian Democrat[2] passed before the Civil War began, and Johnson held himself back by not making the adjustment. He also lacked the guiding hand a president needed when dealing with such contentious issues as the restoration of eleven rebellious states. As a Republican president, he lost an opportunity to work with a Republican Congress because he could not shed his Jacksonian ways.

Andrew Johnson

Another factor leading to Johnson's war with the Radicals involved Abraham Lincoln and the exercise of war powers. Prior to the Civil War Congress represented the people, enacted the laws, and the president seldom vetoed or interfered with the passage of laws. Because of the Civil War, Lincoln stretched executive authority and used power once enjoyed exclusively by Congress.

2. Jacksonian Democrats, named for President Andrew Jackson, advocated increased participation in government by farmers, small-business owners, and other Americans who were not members of the established ruling class.

When the war ended, Lincoln died and Congress reasserted its prewar prerogatives and reclaimed its lost power. The effort resulted in open conflict between the executive and legislative branches of government.

Because the Radicals could muster a two-thirds vote any day of any week, they could write laws and pass them over the veto of the president. Johnson recognized this, but unlike Lincoln, he made little effort to work with Congress to find common ground and strike a compromise. Lincoln understood the importance of working with those in Congress who opposed him, but Johnson never had the opportunity of witnessing Lincoln's methods or of understanding how his predecessor got his way. Instead, Johnson chose to promulgate vetoes that lectured on the Constitution. He failed in his efforts to restore the south because early in his administration he lost the trust of those in Congress who attempted to communicate with him on national issues. The Radicals failed to restore the south because their strategy focused too much on political power and punishment, and not enough on reunifying the southern states in a forgiving and respectful manner.

Samuel "Sunset" Cox, New York City's representative to Congress, spoke of the times as well as anyone when he blamed the Radical Republicans for tearing the Union apart, writing, "What neither secession nor war . . . could do was now done by act of Congress and radical hate. . . . Here began the second contest to save the Union; a contest no less pregnant with the fate of American Institutions, and no less bitterly fought. . . . It took almost a quarter of a century to silence the guns of Moultrie and Sumter."

Poor Statesmanship

Impeachment of a president should never occur in a political atmosphere of good statesmanship. In 1868 statesmanship failed in all three branches of the government. Statesmanship is especially vulnerable to failure when one branch of the government can induce its will on the other two branches. The consequences for a country are never good. Neither Congress, the Supreme Court, nor Johnson as president grew with the times, and when distributing blame, it must fall upon all. Like every political error, it is not the politicians who suffer, it is the people they represent, and neither Johnson, the Radicals, nor the Supreme Court left for the future a good legacy on Reconstruction.

However, Johnson's formula for peaceful reconciliation had merits. Unlike the Radicals, he did not seek political domination of the nation through the smoke screen of civil rights legislation. He foresaw the evils of Reconstruction legislated by Congress and predicted the disastrous outcome. He advocated reconciliation and gradual civil rights legislation, leaving the latter issue to the individual states, as done in the north. He failed as chief executive to alter the policies imposed upon the country by Radical Republicans. Whether Abraham Lincoln could have changed the course of history remains an unanswerable question. The same could be asked of Andrew Johnson. Radical power reigned supreme. It must never be allowed to happen again—in any branch of the government.

Viewpoint 8

"In nearly every respect, . . . the economic policies of Presidential Reconstruction failed."

Johnson's Reconstruction Plan Was a Failure

Eric Foner

The Civil War caused incredible economic devastation in the South. As a result, one of the goals of Reconstruction was to re-shape the southern economy. Eric Foner asserts in the following viewpoint that Andrew Johnson's reconstruction plan was a failure because the president's policies did not lead to economic reform. Foner maintains that Johnson's economic plan failed to encourage northern investment or provide opportunities for black southerners. Foner also notes that Johnson and the other leaders of presidential reconstruction were unable to reform the southern plantation system that had been the basis of the pre-war economy. Foner is a professor of history at Columbia University and the author of numerous books, including *Reconstruction: America's Unfinished Revolution, 1863–1877*, from which this viewpoint has been excerpted.

No one can claim that the complex structure of labor, property, and tax laws enacted in 1865 and 1866 succeeded fully in controlling the black laborer or shaping the evolution of the Southern economy. The "labor shortage" persisted, as did black efforts to resist plantation discipline. The law is an inefficient mechanism for compelling people to work in a disciplined manner. As a South Carolina plantation physician put it, "they can be forced by law *to contract*, but how to enforce their labor is not yet determined." Nonetheless, the legal system of Presidential Reconstruction had profound consequences, limiting the options open to blacks, reinforcing whites' privileged access to economic resources, shielding planters from the full implications of emancipation, and inhibiting the development of a free market in land and labor.

Reshaping the Southern Economy

The aim of resurrecting as nearly as possible the old order with regard to black labor, moreover, contradicted a second purpose of the new governments: reshaping the economy so as to create a New South. Before the war, a small band of modernizers had urged the South to reorient its economy by building railroads and factories alongside the plantations. Although few of these reformers challenged slavery's status as the central feature of the Southern economy, their plans had foundered on the opposition of the planter class. But with abolition accomplished and King Cotton apparently dethroned, the prospect beckoned of a South more fully attuned to nineteenth-century "progress." Northern investment would spur the growth of railroads and factories, immigration would introduce a new spirit of enterprise, and farmers would no longer see their capital frozen in the labor force. The Southern press extolled the idea of expanding the small prewar textile industry so as to utilize cotton locally and provide employment for the thousands widowed and orphaned by the war. Criticisms of the plantation system itself, a minor theme before the war, now blossomed, with calls for a more scientific agriculture based on small farms and diversified crops. "Our large plantations," declared a South Carolina newspaper in 1866, "must be carved up into respectable farms; our water power must be made available in the erection of manufactories; . . . our young men must learn to work." One New South enthusiast, himself a planter, went so far as to advocate a heavy tax on unimproved land, to force owners to cultivate their holdings or place them on the market.

This comprehensive vision of economic change never commanded majority support during Presidential Reconstruction. But governors like James L. Orr, James Johnson, and Robert Patton extolled the virtues of a New South, and found a receptive audience among the former Whigs who dominated politics and eagerly embraced the idea of state-promoted railroad and industrial development as the key to economic modernization. Before the war, most Southern states had assisted railroad development in one way or another, even, in the case of Georgia, building (with government-owned slaves) a railroad itself. Yet the South lagged far behind the rest of the nation in railroad mileage, and most Southern roads remained small, undercapitalized ventures, their primary purpose to transport plantation staples to the coast. Now, a veritable "railroad fever" swept over the region, as states and localities invested funds and expectations in the iron horse. Alabamans believed railroads would unlock the state's mineral resources and create the "identity of feeling" never before shared by the northern and southern parts of the state. Commercially threatened cities like Charleston and Vicksburg saw railroads as panaceas for economic stagnation, while to upcountry towns they offered a share of national commerce, a means of bypassing older port cities and trading directly with the North. Railroads, declared a Mississippi newspaper, would "revive the energies of the people, open up the resources of the State, and put us in the way of growth and general prosperity."

Although the policy of lending the state's credit to promote railroad construction is usually associated with Radical Reconstruction, it in fact originated under the Johnson governments. An act of February 1867, authorizing the state to endorse railroad bonds at the rate of $12,000 for each mile built, formed the basis of subsequent Alabama aid. Texas, whose governor, James Throckmorton, was a longtime railroad developer, chartered sixteen new roads and adopted an aid program even more generous than Alabama's. Simultaneously, legislatures chartered manufacturing, mining, banking, and insurance corporations. And to promote investment in agriculture, states gave the force of law to credit arrangements guaranteeing a first lien on the crop to persons advancing loans or supplies for farming. These early laws avoided the vexing question of priority among creditors by declaring anyone who made advances equally entitled to a lien. Blacks complained that by failing to establish a laborer's lien on the crop, these laws allowed an indebted planter's entire harvest to be seized by creditors, leaving nothing to pay his employees. But the laws' primary purpose, as a former governor of Mississippi explained, was to attract funds to the South by "inspiring confidence on the part of capitalists."

The South's governors also sought, with varying degrees of success, to resist growing demands for debtor relief, fearing "stay laws" would discourage outside investment. The question of debt provoked more division within the white South than any other issue of Presidential Reconstruction, although the class and sectional alignments hardly conformed to a simple pattern. Not a few indebted planters found stay laws appealing, as did other men of property seeking to avoid repaying prewar loans from Northern merchants and financiers. (As a Texas political leader later recalled, "the idea to take it against Northern debts was all right and a part of the war.") Still others believed stay laws would protect planters from employees suing for the payment of wages. Generally, however, the demand for laws "staying" the collection of debts or repudiating them altogether came from upcountry yeomen whose economic independence was threatened by wartime devastation and postwar crop failures.

Attempts to Encourage Investment

From this complex situation emerged a series of laws, varying from state to state, that postponed the collection of debts, "scaled" old debts to take account of the drastic decline in property values, put off court sessions, and exempted a certain amount of land and personal property from seizure. Some represented real victories for debtors, others merely attempted to head off more radical measures like complete repudiation. All, however, evoked considerable protest in the North—no one would invest, wrote a Northern correspondent of Georgia Governor Charles Jenkins, where "stay laws

are made to prevent the collection of debts"—and top state officials moved swiftly to limit their effectiveness. State courts voided
debtor relief laws in Georgia, Mississippi, and South Carolina. Alabama Governor Patton turned a deaf ear to upcountry demands
that he cancel court sessions after the disastrous crop failure of
1866, and North Carolina's Governor Worth denounced stay laws
as "pernicious alike to debtor and creditor," although he was unable to prevent the enactment of several relief measures.

The willingness of courts and governors to risk "considerable
dissatisfaction among the masses" in order to reassure prospective
Northern investors illustrates the depth of their commitment to
economic modernization. In nearly every respect, however, the
economic policies of Presidential Reconstruction failed. The programs of railroad aid accomplished virtually nothing—in the
eleven states of the Confederacy, only 422 miles of track were laid
in 1866 and 1867, none at all in Louisiana, South Carolina, and
Mississippi. Despite the appointment of commissioners of immigration, nearly all the immigrants who entered the country remained in the North and West—the number of foreign-born res-
idents of the eleven Confederate states was lower in 1870 than in
1860. Industrial development remained insignificant. A few establishments, like Richmond's Tredegar Iron Works, attracted enough
Northern investment to resume production, but most Southern
entrepreneurs who ventured north in search of capital returned
home empty-handed. With lucrative opportunities available in the
West, investors had no desire to risk their funds in the South's un-
stable political climate. "Very few persons are willing to trust their
investments in the South," concluded former Massachusetts Governor John Andrew. "It is easier to sell an imaginary copper mine
in Jupiter, than it is to hire ten per cent on the best lands in the
South, on the northern market."

The stillbirth of this early New South program had many causes,
some far beyond the power of Southern politicians to affect. Neither the disastrous economic consequences of the Civil War nor
the legacy of decades of plantation dominance could be erased in
two short years. But in some ways, the failure reflected the divided
mind and contradictory aims of those advocating economic
change. The South's inability to attract immigration illustrates the

problem. Some reformers looked upon newcomers as prospective landowners, whose presence would facilitate the breakup of the plantation system and the rise of modern, market-oriented small farming. Others, however, intended immigration not to undermine the plantation but to preserve it. "Immigration," a prominent North Carolina lawyer wrote in 1865, "would, doubtless, be a blessing to us, provided we could always control it, and make it entirely subservient to our wants." Not surprisingly, European immigrants did not relish the idea of taking the place of blacks as plantation laborers. One Alabama planter brought in thirty Swedes in 1866, housed them in slave cabins and fed them the usual rations. Within a week the laborers had departed, informing him "they were not slaves." To attract immigrants, observed A.B. Cooper, another Alabaman, the South must abandon the idea of labor associated with the plantation: "We must divest ourselves of the idea that we can *command, control* the laborer. We must be prepared to receive him as a free man, an equal, and treat him as such."

Dissolving the Plantation System

Cooper grasped an important fact. Just as the realities of a political economy dominated by slavery frustrated efforts at agricultural reform before the war, so genuine postwar modernization would have required an assault on the plantation. Throughout the world, plantation societies are characterized by persistent economic backwardness. Geared to producing agricultural staples for the world market, they have weak internal markets, and planter classes use their political power to prevent the emergence of alternative economic enterprises that might threaten their control of the labor force. Because they failed to come to grips with the plantation itself, the leaders of Presidential Reconstruction lacked a coherent vision of Southern progress. They wanted the trappings of economic development without accepting its full implications—an agrarian revolution and a free labor market. Newspapers that called for breaking up the plantations in the same breath demanded strict legislation immobilizing black labor. Laws intended to modernize the Southern economy coincided with measures, enacted by the same legislatures, to discipline the plantation labor force. Taxes on property remained so low that the establishment of public schools or other forward-looking social services became impossible.

At least the planter class possessed the virtue of consistency; it had no intention of presiding over its own dissolution. It would support railroads, factories, and Northern investment so long as these supplemented and invigorated the plantation and did not threaten the stability of the black labor force. Those who spoke of dismantling the plantations had no idea what would become of the black population. The entire New South program, in fact, assumed that substitutes would be found for black labor. Scientific agriculture and the introduction of machinery would enable large estates to "dispense with the services of freedmen" altogether. Family labor would suffice for small farms. Reformers spoke of factories employing white laborers, and of small farms tilled by white newcomers replacing black belt plantations, without making any provision for the former slaves, apart from morbid predictions that they would conveniently "die out." Certainly, spokesmen for a New South had no intention of seeing the finest land in the region fall into black hands.

The entire experience of Presidential Reconstruction reveals how profoundly attitudes toward the emancipated slaves and their place in the new social order affected efforts to reshape the Southern polity and economy. The unwillingness of unconditional Unionists to broaden their political base to include the freedmen necessitated the massive disenfranchisement of former Confederates, exacerbating hatreds generated by the Civil War and tainting border governments with illegitimacy. Andrew Johnson's obsession with keeping blacks in order led inevitably to abandonment of the idea of destroying planters' economic and political hegemony. And the inability of the leaders of the governments he created to conceive of blacks as anything but plantation laborers doomed the idea of real economic reform. In the end, their policies envisioned less a New South than an improved version of the old.

CHAPTER 3

The New Social Order

# Chapter Preface

Reconstruction created a new social order, one in which southern blacks had opportunities that had been denied them prior to the Civil War. One of these opportunities was the chance to own land and earn money off that land, thus enabling blacks to play an important economic role in the postwar South—not as slaves putting money in their masters' coffers, but as freedmen who could provide for their own families. Although some southern blacks who were not slaves had been property owners prior to the Civil War, land was now available to those who had been slaves. However, the antipathy of many white politicians, particularly President Andrew Johnson, and economic exploitation prevented many blacks from achieving their dream of becoming successful landowners.

Efforts to provide southern blacks with property actually began several months before the end of the Civil War. Union army general William Tecumseh Sherman issued Special Field Order 15 on January 16, 1865. The order created an exclusive settlement for blacks on the Sea Islands (located off the Georgia coast) and a thirty-mile piece of land along the coast of Charleston, South Carolina. Black families that moved to these areas would be given forty acres of property and an army mule—hence, the phrase "forty acres and a mule." With the assistance of the Freedmen's Bureau, an agency whose responsibilities included supervising and managing southern lands confiscated by the Union army during the Civil War nearly ten thousand black families settled on 400,000 acres of that settlement by June 1865.

Further attempts to make blacks landowners increased after the war. In 1866 Congress passed the Southern Homestead Act, which opened public lands in Alabama, Mississippi, Louisiana, Arkansas, and Florida to all settlers regardless of race. Settlers could purchase up to eighty acres of land at low prices in exchange for living on and cultivating the land for five years. In addition, several freedmen's aid societies purchased southern land and resold it in small lots to freedmen. These actions helped lead to a significant rise in the number of black landowners. According to Loren Schweninger, a professor of history at the University of North Carolina at Greensboro, the number of black owners increased tenfold between 1860 and 1870, from 16,172 to 168,034.

Despite the spike in land ownership, blacks often found themselves not only unable to acquire property but forced to return their land—devastating blows to a people hoping to gain economic independence. President Johnson played a major role in thwarting the hopes of blacks. His Proclamation of Amnesty, issued on May 29, 1865, stated that former Confederates who had been pardoned could recover lands that had been occupied or confiscated by the Union army. Consequently, many of the newly landed freedmen had to return their property to the people who used to be their slave masters. As James M. McPherson explains in *Ordeal by Fire: The Civil War and Reconstruction*: "By 1866, nearly all the arable land once controlled by the Freedmen's Bureau had been returned to its ex-Confederate owners."

In spite of its passage of the Southern Homestead Act, the legislative branch also made it difficult for blacks to create a new social order. In February 1866 Congress defeated a bill that would have given 3 million acres of public land in Florida, Mississippi, Alabama, Louisiana, and Arkansas to freed slaves and white southern refugees who had been loyal to the Union. In his argument against the bill, Democratic representative Burwell C. Ritter contended that the proposed legislation was unconstitutional and would drive whites out of the affected states. According to Ritter, "It is not to be expected that the two races will live contentedly where there are large numbers of the colored people living near to neighborhoods settled with white persons." Another blow to black land ownership occurred when Republican representative Thaddeus Stevens's 1867 land reform bill, that would have provided male adult freed slaves with forty-acre parcels and one hundred dollars to build a home, was defeated.

Economic exploitation further stymied potential landowners. In his book *The Reconstruction of the Nation*, Rembert W. Patrick states: "Unscrupulous men capitalized on the Negro's desire for land by selling him colored stakes to mark the corners of his future grant. Many illiterates hung hopefully to an official-looking paper, believing it to be a deed when in reality its words described how four dollars had been lifted from the victim." Another way in which blacks were exploited was through the sharecropping and share-renting systems. Under the first arrangement, black croppers provided labor in exchange for land, housing, and half the crop as payment. Share renters also furnished their own livestock, seeds, and tools. David Blight, in his essay "The Age of Emancipation," explains that freedmen accepted the sharecropping system "because it appeared to provide a degree of autonomy over their economic lives. . . . But this system evolved into debt dependency for most sharecroppers." Tenants often went into debt if their lands brought forth a low yield or if crop prices fell. Sharecroppers found themselves indebted to country merchants (who were quite often the plantation owners themselves), who as monopolies could set prices as high as they liked. Many blacks found themselves too impoverished to retain their lands. Blight notes that by 1900, blacks owned only 2 percent of farms although they were more than 50 percent of the southern population.

Although the new social order that Reconstruction created opened up opportunities such as land ownership that most blacks had not previously enjoyed, it fell far short of placing blacks on an equal economic, social, and political footing with whites. The authors in the following chapter debate the new social order brought forth during Reconstruction.

Viewpoint 1

"We ask a right to all the different boxes—to the witness-box, the jury-box, and the ballot-box."

Blacks Should Have the Right to Vote

Frederick Douglass

Frederick Douglass was a former slave, prominent abolitionist, and the leading spokesperson for African Americans during the nineteenth century. As a staunch supporter of civil liberties for African Americans, he often spoke in support of giving blacks the right to vote. In the following speech, given in Philadelphia in September 1866, Douglass asserts that African Americans have earned the right to suffrage because of their efforts in helping the North win the Civil War and because they are eager to participate in American society and politics. Douglass also contends that as a democracy, the United States must permit universal suffrage. On March 30, 1870, Congress ratified the Fifteenth Amendment, which gave African American men the right to vote.

I am going to speak to you of the claims of the negro. Perhaps it is hardly necessary, when you are up to this point, but for the sake of some who hear and who stand by let me say a word on behalf of that great principle of human equality . . . as applied to the black race.

Frederick Douglass, address delivered in Philadelphia, Pennsylvania, September 4, 1866.

What the War Settled

Some things have been settled, fellow-citizens, by the [civil] war, by the tremendous conflict which has at last subsided. Some things have been settled concerning my race, and one of the things settled is this, that the negro will fight. We have been accustomed to regard him as a natural born Christian—so well born that he needed not to be born again; that if smitten on one cheek he would turn the other also; but the late war has decided that he would fight. I always knew he would fight or thought I knew it; and the only reason why he has not demonstrated his ability to fight heretofore is, that the negro is not only a natural born Christian, but he is a philosopher—he is a thinker. The only reason he has not fought before is because he had no reasonable probability of whipping anybody. As soon as he was convinced that there was the slightest shadow of hope, he was ready to bare his bosom to the storm of war and to face the enemy, with a valor scarcely inferior, if inferior at all, to the very best troops we have marshalled against the foe. It is settled he can fight and will fight.

Another thing is settled. It is settled that he is a permanent part of the American people. That he is here and that no scheme of colonization or no mode of extirpation can be adopted by which he shall be entirely eradicated from this land. He is here. I know that there are certain ethnological statesmen who are predicting his disappearance from the republic; that he will die out like the Indian. But they forget an important fact—that their simile, if it is to be called a simile, lacks similarity, lacks likeness. There is no resemblance in the elements that go to make up the character of a civilized man between the Indian and the negro. The one, too stiff to bend, breaks. The one refuses your civilization, rejects it. He looks upon your towns and your cities, your villages, your steamboats, and your canals and railways and electric wires, and he regards them with aversion. He sees the ploughshare of your civilization tossing up the bones of his venerated fathers, and he retreats before the onward progress of your civilization. He retreats from the Atlantic to the lakes, from the lakes to the great rivers, and disappears finally on the western slope of the Rocky Mountains. While he remains here he disdains your civilization; he abhors your fashions, he refuses to adopt them.

But not so with the negro. He accepts them; he rejoices in them; he adopts your religion; he adopts your political ideas; he receives willingly your mode of government; he incorporates himself naturally with your civilization. More unlike you than the Indian in form and in features, but incomparably more like you in all the elements that go to make up civilized man than the Indian. Against him there is a prejudice; against the Indian none. There is a romantic reverence—a sort of hero-worship—paid the Indian all over this country; while the negro is despised; yet the Indian rejects your civilization, and the negro accepts it. He is with you, of you, been here for the last two hundred and fifty years, braving the same latitudes, longitudes and altitudes in facing the same climate; enduring hardships that well might exterminate another people, yet living, flourishing with you, accepting all that is valuable in your civilization and serving you at every turn.

Will Not Be Sent Away

It was said by [Irish politician] Daniel O'Connell twenty years ago that "the history of Ireland might be traced like a wounded man through a crowd by his tracks of blood." Incomparably more truthfully may this statement be made respecting the negro. For two hundred and fifty years we have been subjected to all the exterminating forces of slavery—marriage abolished, organization unknown, if more than five meet together, stripes, education denied, the right to learn to read the name of the God that made us denied, the family tie broken up—yet under it all, under all the exterminating forces of slavery here we are to-day, and an Uncle Tom in the church, and a Robert Small [sic] in the harbor of Charleston.[1] Well my friends, we shall not be sent away, because there is nobody to send us away.

We shall not be sent away for another reason, because we are useful to you—useful to the South, useful to the North, useful to the whole country. In time of peace useful as laborers, with whom in that Southern clime no laborers can compete, and useful to you

---

1. Robert Smalls was a slave who piloted the ship *Planter*. He led the slave crew into Union waters and surrendered. He would later become a representative from South Carolina.

in time of war, because we can fight. And America may need both our usefulness [and] our industry as a means of defence against internal and external foes.

Well, fellow citizens, it is about admitted, I suppose, that we are here between four and five millions strong. The question comes at once, shall the presence of this vast black population be made a blessing to themselves and a blessing to us, a blessing to the whole country, or a curse to themselves, a curse to you, and a curse to the whole country? Statesmanship has but one answer. It has given it this morning from the eloquent lips of Senator [Richard] Yates. Philanthropy has but one answer, and it has given

Congress ratified the Fifteenth Amendment in 1870, which granted African American men the right to vote.

it from a thousand pulpits and a thousand platforms to-day. It is this, the thorough and complete incorporation of the whole black element into the American body politic. Anything less than this will prove an utter failure in my judgment.

You want me to speak my honest sentiments? We ask a right to all the different boxes—to the witness-box, the jury-box, and the ballot-box. I tell you we want that box, for all in that box are certainly secure. We ought to ask for that especially. Anybody out of it are in a bad box. I ask it because the negro is a man, and we have recently become aware that a great revolution is going on—a great political revolution in the United States. It is for manhood suffrage. All that can be urged in the face of any man's right to vote, can be urged as to his right to vote, no matter what his color. We want it not only because we are men, [but] because of what we are here in this country especially. In a monarchical, aristocratic or autocratic [government] it is a burden which is easy to be borne by the masses, for the burden is distributed over a vast number of individuals, leaving but a small portion to each individual; and besides the masses of men in all communities can take care of themselves. When they move, thrones, dominations, principalities and powers tremble and have to give way; when they move, crowns and coronets are rent; when they move, they must be respected.

We have heard from Downing St[reet] how the good people of Old England assembled in Hyde Park to assert their right to suffrage. They were not black people, but white men who assembled there to assert their right to suffrage, and the people, in the majesty of their might, rose when the Government would prevent them and declared that they would meet—they did meet. Downing St[reet] turned pale. It would have cost the privileged classes of Old England dearly if they had insisted on preventing the assemblage.

I go for this right because our Government is a democratic one; because it is based upon the principle of universal suffrage; and the right cannot be denied on account of complexion.

And I have another argument. It is this—the black man has deserved it. I do not say that the black man has fought any better than the white man in the last great war. I do not mean to say that you could not have put down the rebellion without him, for I believe you could. The whole people of the North were able to end it, to put down all the slave masters of the South. But this I do say, while I do not say that you could not go it alone—the negro helped you to put it down. They were your friends, too. They helped your escaping prisoners from Southern dungeons—Andersonville, Belle Isle and Castle Thunder. And all I ask you to remember in this Convention [is] that you may want them again.

Viewpoint 2

"The negroes are not the equals of white Americans, and are not entitled by any right, natural or acquired, to participate in the Government of this country."

Blacks Should Not Have the Right to Vote

Benjamin M. Boyer

In 1866 only five states allowed black men full suffrage. Seeking to expand African American voting rights, Radical Republicans sponsored a bill that would enfranchise blacks living in the District of Columbia.

Benjamin M. Boyer, a Democratic representative from Pennsylvania, was one of the politicians who spoke out against the bill. In Boyer's opinion, Radical Republicans misinterpreted Thomas Jefferson's declaration that "all men are created equal." According to Boyer, the Founding Fathers and the authors of several state constitutions had no intention of extending suffrage to African Americans. He also asserts that granting black men the right to vote would be unwise because African Americans are biologically inferior to white people.

Benjamin M. Boyer, address before the United States House of Representatives, Washington, DC, January 10, 1866.

The District of Columbia bill passed the House of Representatives, but Republicans caused the bill to die in a Senate committee.

It is proposed by this bill to confer the elective franchise upon the colored population of the District of Columbia, and to elevate at once, without any qualification or preparation, a heterogeneous mass of about thirty thousand negroes and mulattoes to a complete political equality with the white inhabitants. It is proposed to do this, too, in opposition to the known wishes of a large majority of the citizens of the District, and in the face of an election held here only a few days ago in which the vote against negro suffrage was nearly unanimous. . . .

It would ill become us to fasten, by our votes, upon the people of this District, against their consent, a measure which the people of our own States have already pronounced a political degradation, and have provided against its infliction upon *them* by constitutional enactments. In eighteen out of twenty-five States now represented in this Congress negroes and mulattoes are not allowed to vote. In some of the others there are special restrictions imposed. In three of the States—Connecticut, Wisconsin, and Minnesota—elections were recently held, in which the people by heavy majorities decided against negro suffrage. Yet in each of the States the number of colored persons is comparatively small, while here it probably equals one third of the entire population. In all the States the people have settled this question for themselves, and I claim the same privilege for the people of the District of Columbia. . . .

A White Man's Government

But we were told the other day by my distinguished colleague, the chairman of the committee on reconstruction, [Mr. Thaddeus Stevens,] that "to say so is political blasphemy." And in support of his position he said further that "our fathers repudiated the whole doctrine of the legal superiority of races." But the truth is too plain for discussion, that our fathers recognized and practiced directly the opposite doctrine, and even fortified by the bulwarks of the Constitution itself the subjection of the inferior race. No man can read with open eyes and candid mind the Constitution of the United States, as made by our fathers, and fail to see that this Government was intended by its founders to be a white man's Government. It was on this very account that the early abolitionists denounced it as a covenant with hell, and the advocates of the higher law proposed to trample it under foot.

Arguments derived from the phraseology of the Declaration of American Independence would scarcely need a refutation, were it not for the pertinacity with which they are thrust upon us. If, however, by the expression therein contained, that "all men are created free and equal," we are to infer that the illustrious slave-holders who helped to frame that instrument intended to assert the political equality of the races, we must believe also the monstrous anomaly that they intended to proclaim their daily life a continuous lie and their supremacy over the negro a most atrocious and wicked usurpation. If so, what blasphemy would have been their appeal to the Supreme Judge of the world for the rectitude of their intentions, and what mockery to profess as they did a decent respect for the opinions of mankind. . . .

We find in the constitutions of many of the States the same words so much dwelt upon by the advocates of negro equality; and further on in the same constitutions we find words expressly including the negro from all participation in the government.

The constitution of Connecticut, adopted in 1818, says, "that all men, when they form a social compact, are equal in rights; and that no men or set of men are entitled to exclusive public emoluments or privileges in the community." But this declaration did not prevent the insertion of a clause in the same instrument confining the elective franchise to the *white* male citizens of the State.

Mr. Speaker [Schuyler Colfax], in the constitution of your own State of Indiana, adopted as late as 1851, I find these same talismanic words, "All men are created equal." But further on in the same constitution I find these other words, "No negro or mulatto shall have the right of suffrage." And in another place these additional words, "No negro or mulatto shall come into or settle in the State after the adoption of this constitution." And this last prohibition is enforced by heavy pains and penalties. Surely it will not be pretended that the intelligent people of Indiana intended to make a public proclamation of their injustice by asserting the equality of the negro, while by their organic law they denied to him all the rights of an equal, and even a home within the limits of their community.

In the constitution of the State of Oregon, adopted in 1857, there are these words: "We declare all men, when they form a social compact, are equal in rights." But in the same instrument we find also these other words, "No negro, Chinaman, or mulatto shall have the right of suffrage."

And Kansas, too, in her constitution, adopted in 1859, declares "that all men are possessed of equal and inalienable rights." But by the constitution of Kansas white male persons alone can vote.

In the constitution of the State of Iowa, adopted in 1857, are contained these words: "All men are by nature free and equal." But whether the right of suffrage should be confined to whites was submitted to a vote of the people of the State, and they decided that in that State white persons alone should vote. Yet the whole colored population of Iowa at that time did not exceed a thousand. . . .

Not Completely Equal

All men have indeed in some sense been created equal; but to apply this in its broadest signification, so as to ignore all national and ethnological inequalities among men, would involve the grossest absurdity. All men were endowed by their Creator with the equal right to receive, to do, and to enjoy according to their several capacities and in subservience to the common good. All men are equally entitled by nature to the enjoyment of "life, liberty, and the pursuit of happiness," but it does not follow from this that different races of men can all enjoy these blessings together in the same community and in the same form of government upon terms of complete equality. If it be true, as is affirmed by the greatest of the Apostles, that "God hath made of one blood all the nations of men," the same high authority informs us also that "he hath determined the bounds of their habitation." There is one extensive region of the earth where, all things considered, the negro is the superior of the white man, and where his race, defended by natural laws, has successfully defied the invading legions of conquering Rome and all the efforts of European enterprise. In

Ethiopia the negro is and must ever continue to be the ruling race. But laws of Providence as imperative as those which have set apart Ethiopia for *him* will in the end preserve this Government for white men and their posterity, notwithstanding all the morbid excitements of this hour and all the temporary evils to which they are likely to lead. The ordinances of nature are not to be repealed by acts of Congress.

Of the same nature as the argument just answered is the one derived from that clause in the Constitution of the United States which guarantees to all the States a republican form of government. Strangely enough, it is insisted that to make a State republican in form its negro population must vote. But of this principle the founders of our Republic must surely have lived and died in blissful ignorance, for they certainly acted and talked as if they imagined they were living in republican communities, even when surrounded by negro slaves. If the negro has a natural right to vote because he is a human inhabitant of a community professing to be republican, then women should vote, for the same reason; and the New England States themselves are only *pretended* republics, because their women, who are in a considerable majority, are denied the right of suffrage.

Some of the reformers do say that after the negro will come the women. But I protest against this inverse order of merit; and if both are to vote I claim precedence for the ladies. There is one sense in which I will admit that negro votes will be needed at the South to make *Republican* States. And that is the sense in which the term "Republican" was used by my colleague [Mr. Thaddeus Stevens] in his speech already referred to, when, with even more than his characteristic candor, he assigned a reason for the coercion of southern communities into the adoption of negro suffrage. Said he:

> If they should grant the right of suffrage to persons of color, I think there would always be Union white men enough in the South aided by the blacks to divide the representation, and thus continue the Republican ascendency.

But I deny that to be the precise form of republican government guarantied by the Constitution.

An Inferior Race

It is common for the advocates of negro suffrage to assume that the *color* of the negro is the main obstacle to his admission to political equality; and the gentleman from Iowa [Mr. James F. Wilson] dwelt long upon that argument. But it is not the complexion of the negro that degrades him, and I grant that it is but a shallow argument that goes no deeper than his skin. If he is to be excluded from equality in the Government it is not because he is black, nor because he has long heels and woolly hair, nor because the bones of his cranium are thick and inclose a brain averaging by measurement fewer cubic inches in volume than the skulls of white Americans, (although that fact is significant,) nor because of his odor, (although that is not always agreeable,) nor because his facial outline does not conform to our ideas of beautiful humanity. All these considerations I am willing to discard from the argument. But if the peculiarities I have mentioned are the outward badges of a race by nature inferior in mental caliber, and lacking that vim, pluck, and pose of character which give force and direction to human enterprise, and which are essential to the safety and progress of popular institutions, then the negroes are not the equals of white Americans, and are not entitled by any right, natural or acquired to participate in the Government of this country.

Viewpoint 3

"The civil-rights bill I regard as a just and righteous measure which this Government must adopt in order to guarantee to all citizens equal rights."

A Federal Civil Rights Bill Is Necessary

Richard H. Cain

On March 13, 1866, Congress passed the Civil Rights Act, which declared that anyone born in the United States is a citizen entitled to full constitutional rights. In May 1870 Massachusetts senator Charles Sumner, one of the most powerful Radical Republicans in American politics, started a campaign for broader civil rights legislation because he believed that the 1866 bill failed to prevent discrimination toward blacks. Sumner died on March 11, 1874, before he could see the passage of a second civil rights law. However—perhaps in homage to their influential comrade—the Senate approved a civil rights bill on May 23, 1874, that prohibited racial discrimination in schools, churches, hotels, restaurants, theaters, cemeteries, and public transportation.

Richard H. Cain, a black congressman from South Carolina, was one of the leading supporters of the legislation in the House of Representatives. In a speech delivered on February 3, 1875, Cain asserts that the House should support the Civil Rights Act because American government is based on the principle that all men born in the United States are entitled to all the rights of cit-

Richard H. Cain, address before the United States House of Representatives, Washington, DC, February 3, 1875.

izenship. He also argues that southern opposition to the bill is based on the false claim that northerners, in particular Republicans, are trying to stir up strife among the different races and classes. In Cain's opinion, southerners are to blame for any racial problems that exist in the United States—problems that would be solved by the passage of the act.

The House of Representatives approved a modified form of the bill—one that eliminated the provisions that required the integration of schools, churches, and cemeteries—on February 5, 1875. The Senate approved the new bill on February 27. Two days later, President Ulysses S. Grant signed the Civil Rights Act of 1875 into law. However, the Supreme Court declared the act unconstitutional in an 1883 decision.

W hy not pass the civil-rights bill? Are there not five millions of men, women, and children in this country, a larger number than inhabited this country when the fathers made the tea party in Boston harbor, five millions whose rights are as dear and sacred to them, humble though they be, as are the rights of the thirty-odd millions of white people in this land? I am at a loss to understand the philosophy which these gentlemen [white southerners] have learned; how they can arrogate to themselves all rights, all liberty, all law, all government, all progress, all science, all arts, all literature, and deny them to other men formed of God equally as they are formed, clothed with the same humanity, and endowed with the same intellectual powers, but robbed by their connivance of the means of development. I say I am at a loss to understand how they can deny to us these privileges and claim them for themselves.

The civil-rights bill simply declares this: that there shall be no discriminations between citizens of this land so far as the laws of the land are concerned. I can find no fault with that. The great living principle of the American Government is that all men are free. We admit from every land and every nationality men to come here and under the folds of that noble flag repose in peace and protection. We assume that, whatever education his mind may have received, each man may aspire to and acquire all the rights of citizenship. Yet because, forsooth, God Almighty made the face of the negro black, these gentlemen would deny him that right though he be a man. Born on your soil, reared here amid the toils and sorrows and griefs of the land, producing by his long years of toil the products which have made your country great, earnestly laboring to develop the resources of this land, docile though outraged, yet when the gentlemen who held them in bondage—sir, I will not repeat the dark scenes that transpired under the benign influence and direction of that class of men.

He [Virginia representative Thomas Whitehead] tells you that since the liberation of the negro the people of the North want to stir up strife. Why, sir, you of the South stir up the strife. When the Government of the United States had made the black man free; when Congress, in the greatness of its magnanimity prepared to give to every class of men their rights, and in reconstructing the Southern States guaranteed to all the people their liberties, you refused to acquiesce in the laws enacted by Congress; you refused to "accept the situation," to recognize the rights of that class of men in the land. You sought to make the reconstruction acts a nullity, if possible. You sought to re-enslave the black man by every means in your power. You denied the validity of those reconstruction acts which undertook to protect him in his liberty. It is because you thus refused to accept the situation as it ought to have been accepted that there is now strife in the land. And I will tell you further that there will be strife all over this land as long as five millions of black men, women, and children are deprived of their rights. There will be no real and enduring peace so long as the rights of any class of men are trampled under foot, North or South, East or West.

Gentlemen say that the Republican party is keeping up a continual strife among classes. Why, sir, it is not the Republican party that is keeping up strife. The Republican party is seeking to maintain peace. It is the southern men that make the strife, because they will not let us have our liberties, because they seek to thwart the designs of the Government. No man can read the tales of horror now being brought out by the investigating committees in the South, without realizing the fact that it is not the northern people or the Republican party that makes this strife in the country.

I regard it as essential to the peace of the country that there shall be no discrimination between citizens; and the civil-rights bill I regard as a just and righteous measure which this Government must adopt in order to guarantee to all citizens equal rights.

Bad Blood

And, Mr. Speaker, I am astonished that there is an apparent disposition in some quarters to give this question the go-by. "O," gentlemen say, "you will stir up strife in the country"—"bad blood," the gentleman from Virginia said. Well, I think there has been a good deal of "bad blood" in the South already. It seems to me that a few years ago they had some "bad blood" in the South— very bad blood. And if any one will read the transactions in the South during the last few months, he will find that the "bad blood" has not all got out of the South—bad blood stirred up, not by the northern people, but by the southern people themselves.

Now, I do not think there is so much bad blood between the blacks and whites. The gentleman tells us in the next breath that they have the best laborers in the country. Well, if the labor is so good why do you not treat your laborers well? If they are the best class of laborers, if they do so much, why not guarantee to them their rights? If they are good laborers, if they produce your corn and your rice, if they give you such grand products, is it not proper and just that you should accord to them the rights that belong to them in common with other men?

The gentleman said that the slaves lived better than their masters. That is susceptible of grave doubt. I think there is a great difference between hog and hominy in the log cabin and all the luxuries of life in the richly-carpeted mansion. It seems to me there is a great difference when one class bear all the labor and produce all the crops, while the other class ride in their carriages, do all the buying and selling, and pocket all the money.

The gentleman says he wishes to defend "old Virginny." Now I do not think that Virginia is any better than the rest of the States in this respect. My colleague has already stated that they do not allow colored people to ride in the cars except in cars labeled "Colored people allowed in this car." "Old Virginny never tires!" In this connection let me bring another fact to the gentleman's notice. Eight or ten months ago a lady acquaintance of mine was traveling from South Carolina to Washington; she had ridden in a first-class car through North Carolina, having paid a first-class fare; but when she got to the gentleman's noble State of "old Virginny," she was rudely taken and pushed out of the first-class car into the smoking-car, where she was obliged to remain until she passed out of "old Virginny." It is in this way that they give colored people all their rights and privileges in "old Virginny." It seems to me that such things as this must make bad blood for somebody.

But, Mr. Speaker, the gentleman says that this measure is merely an attempt on the part of the people at the North to continue agitation and strife. Sir, I believe that if Congress had boldly passed the civil-rights bill a year ago; if it had let the nation know that the mandates of the highest authority of the land must be obeyed, there would be no trouble to-day about the civil-rights bill, nor about "mixed schools," etc. The laws of the country would be obeyed. The trouble is merely that there has been a disposition to some extent on the part of some republicans to minister to the prejudices of southern men. Why is it that southern men make all this ado about schools? I think, Mr. Speaker, you will find that of all the men who have voted against the civil-rights bill in the contest that has been going on, there have been more men from the South than from the North on the republican side. The trouble arises in that direction.

Viewpoint 4

"The [civil rights] bill ought not to pass; the matter ought to be left to the States."

A Federal Civil Rights Bill Is Not Necessary

Robert B. Vance

The Civil Rights Act of 1866 declared that all African Americans were citizens and forbade states from discriminating on the basis of race. Although the act helped improve the civil rights of blacks, many Republican politicians—most notably Massachusetts senator Charles Sumner—believed that stronger legislation was needed. Sumner proposed a second civil rights bill in 1870, which would ban segregated schools and discrimination in a number of public places. Congress debated the legislation for nearly five years, at the conclusion of which the Civil Rights Act of 1875 became law. However, the approved legislation did not include several of Sumner's original proposals, in particular the ban on segregated schools.

Robert B. Vance, a former Confederate officer and a Democratic representative from North Carolina, spoke out against the proposed legislation on January 10, 1874. Vance explains that he opposes the bill because it seeks to protect social, rather than civil, rights. In the congressman's opinion, while blacks should be al-

Robert B. Vance, address before the United States Congress, Washington, DC, January 10, 1874.

lowed to ride in railway cars and eat in restaurants, which he considers civil rights, no law should force whites to sit with blacks in public places. Such a law would mandate social interaction between blacks and whites and would surely lead to increased antagonism between the races. Vance also argues that integrated schools would destroy the southern school system and lessen the chances that black children would receive an education.

In 1883, the Supreme Court ruled that the Civil Rights Act of 1875 was unconstitutional.

M r. Speaker, having been unable to obtain the floor on the civil-rights bill, I propose to devote a portion of my time to the discussion of that subject; and I think I can do so without prejudice and without subjecting myself truthfully to the charge of hatred toward the colored race. In the will of my grandfather (who was one of those who struggled for liberty upon the heights of King's Mountain) he enjoined it upon his children and his grandchildren to treat kindly the colored people upon the plantation. I hope never to forget a sentiment so noble and so worthy of obedience. In fact, as a southern man, as one who has sympathized from my earliest time of knowledge with the South in all the great principles and struggles which have interested her, I have felt it my duty to advance in every laudable way the interests of the colored race in this country. I have even taught a colored Sunday-school of one hundred and fifty scholars. I have endeavored in every way possible to advance the interests of that race. I feel, therefore, that I can speak upon this subject without prejudice.

The charge has been made against the people of the South that their opposition to such measures as the civil-rights bill has arisen from prejudice and hatred. This charge is unfounded; it is untrue. Before the war—in the days past and gone—in the days when there were four million slaves in the South, the churches of the South sent missionaries into the cotton plantations, and down into the orange groves, and out upon the rolling prairies of Texas. Into all parts of the country where great numbers of colored people were collected the churches sent their missionaries, and held up there the standard of the Cross, instructing them in the sublime principles which relate to questions vastly more important than mere earthly things.

I have yet to meet the southern man (and I thank God for it) who does not in his heart rejoice that the colored man is free. In my intercourse with the people of my own land, in my travels through the "sunny South," I have found the feeling everywhere one of gratitude and thankfulness that the chains of the colored man have been broken; that he is now permitted to walk the earth a free man. . . .

Why, then, do we oppose the civil-rights bill? That is the question; and speaking as I do, and feeling as I speak, without prejudice, I will show what is the real objection to the bill known as the civil-rights bill. I think gentlemen of the House will bear me out when I say the title of the bill we had before us ought to be changed, and made to read thus: "A bill to protect the colored people in their social rights." That is the way it should read.

Now, Mr. Speaker the distinguished gentleman from Massachusetts [Benjamin Butler] laid down the law, and it has not been controverted, that all men are entitled under the law to the right to go to a hotel, to ride in a public railway carriage, to interment, and to be taught in the public schools sustained by moneys raised by taxation.

It is laid down as the common law of the land. Now, let us see for a few minutes, Mr. Speaker, how the case stands. There is no railway car in all the South which the colored man cannot ride in. That is his civil right. This bill proposes that he should have the opportunity or the right to go into a first-class car and sit with white gentlemen and white ladies. I submit if that is not a social right. There is a distinction between the two. Now, there is not a hotel in the South where the colored man cannot get entertainment such as food and lodgings. That is his civil right. The bill of the committee provides that there shall be no distinction. Even if he is allowed to go into the dining-room, and is placed at a separate table because of his color, it will be a violation of this law. Placing him, therefore, at the same table with the whites is a social right.

Now, sir, provision has been made for free schools in my own native State of North Carolina. We have cheerfully taxed ourselves there for the education of our people, including the colored race; but separate schools are organized for the instruction of the latter. One of the civil rights of the colored man undoubtedly is the right to be educated out of moneys raised by taxation. His children, under the law, have that right; but this bill goes further, and provides that colored children shall go into the same school with white children, mixing the colored children and the white children in the same schools. I submit to the House whether that is not a social right instead of a civil right. Therefore it is I say this bill ought to be changed, or rather its title ought to be changed. The real objection, then, to civil rights, so called, is that it is not best for both races, that in fact it will be detrimental to the interests of both races.

Damage to Both Races

Now, Mr. Speaker, I propose to show briefly how that will be. In the first place, the true policy in regard to the intercourse of man-

Usurping States' Rights

In 1883 the Supreme Court heard several suits on alleged violations of the Civil Rights Act of 1875. In its decision on these cases, the Court declared that the first two sections of the act—which banned racial discrimination in most public establishments and established penalties for any violations—were unconstitutional because the provisions had not been authorized by either the Thirteenth or Fourteenth Amendments, amendments that ended slavery and gave blacks the right to vote. In the following excerpt from the decision, written by Associate Justice Joseph P. Bradley, the Court argues that the Civil Rights Act has wrongfully entered the domain of local and state governments.

An inspection of the [Civil Rights Act of 1875] shows that it makes no reference whatever to any supposed or apprehended violation of the Fourteenth Amendment on the part of the states. It is not predicated on any such view. It proceeds *ex directo* [di-

kind all over this broad earth is in the recognition of the fact that such intercourse is one made up of mutual interests. It is the interest of the hotel-keeper to entertain his guests, it is the interest of the railway company to transport passengers; the interests are mutual; and that is the true policy all the world over. But whenever you undertake to force persons of color into their social rights, then, in my judgment, you have done the colored man a serious damage. Let the people of the South alone, sir, and this thing will adjust itself. It will come out all right. In coming to this city the other day colored men were sitting in first-class cars with their wives, where they were admitted by the managers of the road; and I am told in this city one of the first hotels admits colored men as guests. It will adjust itself if let alone; but if you undertake to coerce society before it is ready, you will damage the colored man in all his interests, and at the same time do damage to the white race.

There are between four and five millions of colored people in the

rectly] to declare that certain acts committed by individuals shall be deemed offences, and shall be prosecuted and punished by proceedings in the courts of the United States. It does not profess to be corrective of any constitutional wrong committed by the states; it does not make its operation to depend upon any such wrong committed. It applies equally to cases arising in states which have the justest laws respecting the personal rights of citizens, and whose authorities are ever ready to enforce such laws, as to those which arise in states that may have violated the prohibition of the amendment. In other words, it steps into the domain of local jurisprudence, and lays down rules for the conduct of individuals in society towards each other, and imposes sanctions for the enforcement of those rules, without referring in any manner to any supposed action of the state or its authorities.

Justice Joseph P. Bradley, majority opinion in *Declaring the Unconstitutionality of Section 1 and 2 of the Civil Rights Act of March 1, 1875, as Applied to the Several States*, 1883.

South, whose interests are intimately and closely connected with those of the white people. The one cannot well do without the other. Where does the colored man get his place to live, where does he obtain employment? In a great measure from the white men of the country, and almost entirely from those opposed to this bill. And I tell the House now, through you, Mr. Speaker, that the great majority of the people of the Southern States, of all political shades of opinion, are opposed to anything like force in this matter.

Look at my own State, sir. As I went home from the capital during the holidays I met with republican members of the Legislature of North Carolina who stated that we ought to oppose this bill. Republicans do not want it. They think it is wrong. A resolution was introduced into the Legislature of North Carolina in regard to this subject, and it received a very small vote. It did not receive the vote of the republican party. And, sir, it is my opinion that the colored people of the South *en masse* do not want it. They do not want to be brought into apparent antagonism to the white people, because their interests are closely connected together. The colored man cannot do well in the South, he cannot prosper, unless he has the sympathies, unless he has the fostering hand, unless he has the kind care, of the white man extended to him; his interests will suffer if this should not be the case.

And, sir, it is necessary anyhow in this world of ours that there should be kindness running from heart to heart. There has been enough trouble and enough sorrow in this world already. War has stamped its foot upon human sympathies. It has left its scars upon every human heart, sir; and now there ought to be sympathy, there ought to be kindness, there ought to be oneness of interest pervading the whole land. And these people need that thing. You rob the colored man by the passage of this bill more or less of the friendship of the owners of the soil in the South. And you rob him, sir, of the opportunity of education. Gentlemen may treat this statement lightly. The distinguished gentleman from Massachusetts said the other day that he would not act under a threat. He regarded the declaration made here that the schools would be broken up as a threat. It was not a threat, sir, it is a solemn fact.

I ask the attention of the House to this fact: the University of South Carolina was one of the most honored in all the land. That university has turned out some of the most eminent men of this country—Presidents, Senators, governors, and distinguished military chieftains. Where, sir, is it now? In what condition is the University of South Carolina? A law was passed in South Carolina that colored students should be received into that institution. What has been the effect? Some time since there were only from six to nine scholars in the University of South Carolina; while the professors are paid out of moneys raised from the people by taxation. This is no threat, sir. It is a plain, simple truth, that in passing bills of this kind and having mixed schools you destroy the school system of the South. That is to be the effect; and you thereby lessen the chances of the colored children for an education. . . .

Sir, it is absurd for gentlemen to talk about the equality of the races. But let us give to the colored man the opportunity of improvement; let us give him an education. I for one will vote cheerfully and gladly for the appropriation of a portion of the proceeds of the splendid domain of this country for the education of the colored race; but I think it ought to be done in separate schools. Sir, we have already given him the opportunity to be educated; we have allowed him to hold office; we have seen and heard colored men on this floor; they are here now.

The bill ought not to pass; the matter ought to be left to the States. I will not undertake to argue the constitutionality of this question; that has been done by others, and well done. I have only spoken to the effect of the passage of such a measure, and what is best for the interests of both races; and I submit in concluding my remarks that we have really extended to the colored man everything that I think he ought to ask at our hands.

Viewpoint 5

"A brief experience showed us that the negro people were capable of education, with no limit that men could set to their capacity."

Education Will Benefit Southern Blacks

Oliver O. Howard

Few southern blacks had access to education prior to the Civil War; while some slaves learned to read and write, many slave masters forbid such endeavors. However, during Reconstruction, 9 million dollars were spent on schools and teachers for the newly freed slaves. More than half of these funds came from the Freedmen's Bureau, an agency founded in March 1865 to help refugees and freed slaves. In the following viewpoint General Oliver O. Howard, the commissioner of the Freedmen's Bureau, asserts that these new educational opportunities are beneficial to southern blacks. He explains that blacks are capable of becoming educated and are eager to learn. Howard adds that these schools provide training for African Americans who aim to become lawyers, doctors, teachers, and other skilled professionals. He concludes that higher education for freed slaves should be encouraged.

Oliver O. Howard, *Autobiography of Oliver Otis Howard*. New York: Baker and Taylor, 1907.

In my earlier interviews with [Secretary of War Edwin Stanton] in May, 1865, I claimed that the education of the freedmen's children, and of adults, as far as practicable, was *the true relief*.

"Relief from what?" asked Stanton, glancing toward me over his colored glasses.

"Relief from beggary and dependence," I replied.

I had the same opinion with reference to our numerous "white refugees" of the South, though it was believed that they would naturally be incorporated in ordinary schools there without such prejudice to their interests as existed against the negro population.

The Need for Negro Teachers

Very soon all my assistants agreed with me that it would not be long before we must have *negro teachers*, if we hoped to secure a permanent foothold for our schools. This conclusion had become plain from the glimpses already given into Southern society. Naturally enough, the most Christian of the Southern people would prefer to have white teachers from among themselves. Feeling a sympathy for this seeming home prejudice, quite early in 1866, I tried the experiment in one State, in coöperation with the Episcopal Bishop of that State, to put over our school children Southern white teachers, male and female, but the bishop and I found that their faith in negro education was too small, and their ignorance of practical teaching too great, to admit of any reasonable degree of success. After trial and failure it was given up. But faith and enthusiasm combined to give the negro teachers a marvelous progress. Of course, in the outset there were few negroes in the United States who were properly fitted to teach. The most who had a smattering of learning could not speak the English language with a reasonable correctness. It was then a plain necessity to have schools which could prepare teachers. My own sentiment often found vent when I was visited by men of opposite convictions— the one set saying that *no* high schools or colleges were wanted for the freedmen, and the other declaring their immediate and pressing necessity. My own thought favored the latter, but not with haste. It was given in this form: "You cannot keep up the lower grades unless you have the higher." Academies and colleges, universities and normal schools, had long been a necessity in all sections where the free schools had been continuously sustained.

A brief experience showed us that the negro people were capable of education, with no limit that men could set to their capacity. What white men could learn or had learned, they, or some of them, could learn. There was one school diagonally across the street from my headquarters, named the Wayland Seminary. The pupils were from fourteen to twenty years of age. It was taught in 1866 by a lady, who, herself, was not only a fine scholar, but a thoroughly trained teacher. One day the Honorable Kenneth Raynor, of North Carolina, whom I had long known and valued as a personal friend, came to my room to labor with me and show me how unwise were some of my ideas.

He said in substance about this educating the freedmen:

"General Howard, do you not know that you are educating the colored youth above their business? You will only destroy them. Those young girls, for example; they will be too proud or vain to work, and the consequence will be that they will go to dance houses and other places of improper resort."

"Why, my friend," I replied, "do you really think that? I am astonished! That is not the way education affects the Yankee girls. Come with me to the Wayland school, across the street."

Successful Schools

We went together to the large school building and entered the commodious room where the school was just commencing its morning exercises. After extending a pleasant welcome, the teacher gave us seats well back, where we could see the blackboards, which were near her desk, and the open school organ at her left, ready for use. She first sent up two nice-looking girls, of about fifteen years, to the instrument. One played, and the other, like a precentor, led the school in singing. There was evident culture in the singing and playing, and none of the melody was wanting. My friend's eyes moistened; but he whispered: "They always could sing!"

Next, we had a class of reading. It was grateful to cultured ears to have sentences well read and words correctly pronounced. Spelling and defining followed, with very few mistakes. The recitations at the blackboard in arithmetic that next came on were remarkable. To test the pupils beyond their text, I went forward and placed some hard problems there. With readiness and intelligence they were solved. The politeness and bearing of these young people to one another, to the teacher, and to us, struck my good friend with astonishment. Such a school, even of whites, so orderly, so well trained, and so accomplished, Mr. Raynor had seldom seen. As we returned across the street, arm in arm, he said to me: "General, you have converted me!" This fine seminary was tantamount to a normal school. It was preparing many excellent teachers for their subsequent work.

Miss M.R. Mann, a niece of the Honorable Horace Mann, through the aid of Massachusetts friends, had a handsome school building constructed in Washington, D.C., and it had the best possible appliances furnished—all for her own use. She charged tuition, except for those whose purpose was avowed to become teachers. She commenced at the foundation of instruction, and led her pupils step by step on and up, class by class, as high as she could conveniently take them. She began the enterprise in December, 1865. Pupils of different ages were admitted, so that teachers, still in embryo, might learn by experiment. It became before long the model school of the District of Columbia. The neatness and order, the elegant rooms for reciting, and the high grade of Miss Mann's classes in recitations always attracted and surprised visitors. From this school, also, several teachers graduated and proved themselves able and worthy in their subsequent successful career.

There were various other schools, as we know, in the United States which had been long in existence, preparing colored teachers, physicians, ministers, lawyers, and others for the coming needs of the new citizens—notably Oberlin College; Wilberforce University, of Xenia, Ohio; Berea Academy, Kentucky; The Theological Institute (Baptist) at Washington, D.C., and Ashmun Institute at Oxford, Pennsylvania. The institute also for colored youth in Philadelphia, founded in 1837 by the bequest of a Friend, Richard Humphreys, was designed to teach agriculture and mechanical arts, and prepare teachers for their profession. By other gifts, and by the help of benevolent and friendly associations, this institute had come, in 1866, to have a capacity for three hundred

(300) pupils; it was fairly endowed and doing well, giving excellent results. Its teachers were all colored persons. It had that year 48 graduates, 31 of whom became teachers. Still, notwithstanding these sources of supply, the need for more teachers was constant, and if any general system of free schools should be adopted, the demand would be a hundred times beyond the possibility of meeting it by competent instructors.

As the work of carrying forward the schools developed, the old negro clergymen of every name became inadequate for the religious instruction of the more enlightened people. Many ministers felt themselves to be unlearned, and so sought such knowledge of books as they could get. Negro pharmacists and other medical men were soon required, and contentions with white men in the courts demanded friendly advocates at law.

Under the evident and growing necessity for higher education, in 1866 and 1867, a beginning was made. Various good schools of a collegiate grade were started in the South, and normal classes were about this time added, as at Hampton, Charleston, Atlanta, Macon, Savannah, Memphis, Louisville, Mobile, Talladega, Nashville, New Orleans, and elsewhere.

In every way, as commissioner, I now encouraged the higher education, concerning which there was so much interest, endeavoring to adhere to my principle of Government aid in dealing with the benevolent associations. These, by 1867, had broken away from a common union, and were again pushing forward their denominational enterprises, but certainly, under the [Freedmen's] Bureau's supervision, nowhere did they hurtfully interfere with one another.

Each denomination desired to have, here and there, a college of its own. Such institutions the founders and patrons were eager to make different from the simple primary or grammar schools; these, it was hoped and believed, would be eventually absorbed in each State in a great free school system. The educators naturally wished to put a moral and Christian stamp upon their students, especially upon those who would become instructors of colored youth. My own strong wish was ever to lay permanent substructures and build thereon as rapidly as possible, in order to give as many good teachers, professional men, and leaders to the rising generation of freedmen as we could, during the few years of Governmental control.

Viewpoint 6

"We see every day around us the bad effects of improper education of negroes."

Education Will Not Benefit Southern Blacks

George Fitzhugh

Southern slaves had few, if any, educational opportunities. However, thousands of schools for freed slaves and their children were built during Reconstruction. In the following viewpoint George Fitzhugh, a writer and former agent of the Freedmen's Bureau—a government department established in March 1865 to assist refugees and newly freed slaves—argues that educating blacks is both unnecessary and harmful. He asserts that a literary education makes blacks discontented, miserable, and unfit for bodily labor, which Fitzhugh contends is the only employment to which they are suited. According to Fitzhugh, education is a luxury that freed slaves cannot afford and that southern whites should not support.

Educate negroes? Surely: educate them from early childhood for all those industrial pursuits for which they are adapted. But

George Fitzhugh, "The Freedman and His Future: A Rejoinder," *Lippincott's Magazine*, vol. 5, February 1870, pp. 191–97.

don't attempt to make carpenters, or manufacturers, or house-servants, or hostlers, or gardeners of the men, nor seamstresses, nor washerwomen, nor cooks, nor chambermaids of the women. They are too slow, too faithless, too unskillful to succeed in such pursuits when brought in competition with whites. But they are admirably adapted—better adapted than white men—for field-work (in which two-thirds of the white population of the earth are, from dire necessity, engaged), also for working on railroads and canals, for wood-cutting, and for coal and iron mining. Educate them (the full-blooded negroes) for these pursuits, and they will be the most happy, useful and productive population in the world.

Education Could Destroy the Negros

From infancy I have lived where the black population exceeded the white by two to one. From long observation and tedious study I think I have learned to comprehend the nature of the savage or uncivilized race. In one material and all-controlling respect it differs wholly from that of the whites. All savages are CONTENTED—all Caucasians DISCONTENTED. Content begets *vis inertia* of mind and body with the savage, and therefore he can never improve, accumulate property, or acquire that dominion over his fellow-beings which results in slavery to capital; which so-called yet miscalled slavery alone begets, sustains and advances civilization.

So long as savage nature continues (and literary education intensifies and increases it, for even among the whites literary men are remarkable for that *insouciance* or improvidence which is the distinguishing characteristic of the savage), so long as negroes are *contented*, they will have no property, no useful arts, no separate ownership of lands, no law, little or no government, and indeed none of the institutions of civilized life. They are by necessity of nature all equals, all paupers, all ignorant, all wasteful, generous, amiable and improvident—all communists and agrarians; yet, properly taken care of and provided for by the whites, and educated to proper industrial pursuits, they become the most valuable part of every population, because the most productive. To teach them to read, write, cipher, etc., and then to throw them, unprotected, into free competition with the selfish, avaricious, designing, cheating white race, is all that their peculiar friends, North and South, propose.

The common laborer, be he black or white, slave or freeman, is the most valuable of all "live stock." We take care of—nay, we love—our blooded horses, our blooded cattle, our blooded hogs. Should we not more love, more take care of, the amiable and generous negro, who is more valuable than they, and is, besides, our fellow-man? The English understand this thing, and during the dearth of employment for cotton operatives occasioned by our late war they provided amply and munificently for those operatives. We must provide for the negroes in infancy, in old age, in sickness and in winter, for Nature unfits them to provide for themselves. By diminishing their wages we can effect this purpose without loss to ourselves—in fact, only compelling them, in this way, to take care of themselves. The negroes are now fast diminishing in numbers, and will slowly die out entirely if we continue to teach them what is useless to them, and neglect to teach them, and compel them to learn, those arts and pursuits for which they are alone fitted.

Human equality, established and enforced by law in despite of Nature, between inferior and superior races, is the most cruel engine of torture that the wit of man could possibly invent. Hear

Students listen to a lesson in Charleston, South Carolina. African American schools sparked controversy among southerners during Reconstruction.

what Mr. [Horace] Greeley said, twenty years ago, of such equality or free competition even in New York, where there is no inferior race: "Briefly, it seems to me if some malignant spirit had undertaken to contrive a social framework which should subject the poor, the humble, the ignorant to the greatest possible amount and variety of temptations—which should virtually constrain many and irresistibly draw far more to the ways of dissipation and sin—he could hardly, in the light of Christianity and of such civilization as we have, devise anything more admirably adapted to his purpose than the social system under which we now live." Now, every word of this is strictly and accurately true when society is composed of inferior and superior races, but not true as to white society in New York, of which Mr. Greeley is treating.

The immense public and private charities of New York ward off or greatly mitigate the otherwise intolerable evils of free competition, which rages there more fiercely than anywhere else. With all her faults and failings, New York City is one of the most desirable residences for rich and poor in the world, and hence the mighty immigration that is continually pouring into her. New York is not the Devil's work, for New York made Mr. Greeley in fortune, fame and character, and he is a kind-hearted, humane man, a philosopher, a scholar and an ornament to his country—a little wild, however, about negroes and Fourierism. [Charles Fourier (1772–1837), a French utopian socialist, who provided the model for a number of communitarian experiments, including Brook Farm in Massachusetts.]

Better Treatment by Southerners

When mistaken philanthropy has demoralized the negroes by making indifferent scholars of them, and thereby unfitting them for bodily labor—when by educating negro teachers it has diffused the poison of insubordination, of idleness and theft far and wide through the land—when free-love and concubinage have taken the place of lawful marriage, and the negroes are turned over to us Southrons to manage—we will institute a wholly different system. We will encourage the negroes to labor in the fields, give them good wages, comfortable houses, plenty of wholesome food; or, if they will not thus labor, leave them to starve. We Southrons from time immemorial have been kind, humane, generous and tender-hearted.

Let not our Northern friends, then, fear to turn the freedmen over to us. It is our interest to treat them well, and our feelings and sympathies coincide with our interests. We see every day around us the bad effects of improper education of negroes. Those who when slaves were accustomed to field-work are better laborers than ever, and are contented, honest and doing well. Those brought up as house-servants, mechanics, etc., are half their time out of employment, thievish, half starved and discontented. Negro aristocracy in the South is dead, and can never be revived. The pampered menials of *ante-bellum* days have become ragged, starving mendicants and thieves. . . .

Education Does Not Lead to Wealth

There was a high civilization and much wealth in Europe and Western Asia long anterior to the invention of letters. Homer, the greatest of authors, knew not a letter in the book. His works conclusively show that the useful and ornamental arts were generally known and successfully practiced long before his time—in fact, immemorially—by the white race. His exquisite description of the fabrication of the shield of Achilles would, if it stood alone, prove that the mechanic arts have gained nothing by the use of letters; whilst his own works go far to sustain the opinion of Plato, that the human mind has been enfeebled by the invention of letters. But Homer's works are not the only evidences of the superiority of the illiterate ancients in the mechanic arts, thousands of architectural remains, older than the invention and use of a phonetic alphabet, show that architecture has declined just as literature has advanced.

But to descend to our own times and to come nearer home, very many Virginia overseers could neither read nor write, yet they managed farms and negroes much more judiciously and profitably than Mr. Thomas Jefferson or any other scholar, philosopher or agricultural chemist. Too much learning had not taken away their common sense or run them mad. Many men around us, who can neither read nor write, have made handsome properties as farmers, many such as captains of vessels, and a few even as merchants. Nothing so incapacitates a man for making money as profound and various learning. Literature is a luxury in which the poor cannot afford to indulge. Teach negroes to earn their bread and make money, and when they have done so leave them to learn their alphabet if they be fools enough to do so.

Ce n'est que le premier pas qui coute. [it is only the first step that costs.] The over-sanguine, visionary friends of the ignorant negro, half conscious of this fact, propose to omit the *first step*, which the negro's nature inhibits him, and will ever inhibit him, from taking, and leap at once to the second. To make, to amass and to wield capital is the first step in the road to civilization. A literary education is sure to succeed this step. Reverse the order of nature and teach the negro first to read, and then start him to learn to labor and to make money by hand-work, and he will find that his school education unfits him to compete with those who have been working with their hands all the while he was at school. He will find his wants increased, and his ability to supply them diminished. He will be thrown upon the world a miserable, discontented, aspiring, idle, helpless, hopeless thief and vagrant. This picture is not overdrawn. We see around us, every day and every hour, the pauperism and wretchedness that false education entails on negroes; and with them all education is false that attempts to teach them other than the coarsest, commonest and hardest labor. Employed at such labor alone, they will prove themselves our most useful, valuable and productive citizens.

I have seen the circus-horse Champion dance. He danced most infamously, but without doubt his education had cost him ten thousand lashes. Negroes sometimes learn to read about as well as Champion danced, for their organs of speech are as unfitted for reading as the horse's legs for dancing. Yet to acquire a little reading they probably suffer "more pangs and fears than wars or women have." The cruelty of a circus education does not exceed the cruelty of the successful literary education of negroes. And *cui bono?* [For whose advantage?]

Viewpoint 7

"It is remarkable that despite regional variations, . . . significant numbers of freedmen became property owners during [Reconstruction]."

Reconstruction Improved the Economic Status of Southern Blacks

Loren Schweninger

In the following viewpoint, Loren Schweninger asserts that the economic status of southern blacks, as measured by land and property ownership, improved significantly after the Civil War. According to Schweninger, southern African Americans—primarily former slaves—increased their land ownership by as much as 744 percent during the 1860s. He explains that economic growth occurred in both rural and urban areas and was influenced by a variety of factors, including increased black political power, the end of the plantation system, and the rising demand for black workers in the urban lower South. Schweninger is a professor of history at the University of North Carolina at

Loren Schweninger, "Black Economic Reconstruction in the South," *The Facts of Reconstruction: Essays in Honor of John Hope Franklin*, edited by Eric Anderson and Alfred A. Moss Jr. Baton Rouge: Louisiana State University Press, 1991. Copyright © 1991 by Louisiana State University Press. Reproduced by permission.

Greensboro and the author of several books, including *Black Property Owners in the South, 1790–1915*.

Following emancipation, former slaves confronted many obstacles in their efforts to become economically self-sufficient: the legacy of bondage, lack of assistance from federal and state authorities, the hold of whites on the land (especially in the lower South), the emergence of the Ku Klux Klan and other terrorist groups, and a host of economic problems—floods, crop failures, lack of credit, scarcity of money, wartime destruction, and increased competition in towns and cities from various immigrant groups. Yet the freed slaves viewed their new status as one of opportunity. Most blacks rejected working on the plantation in gangs, as they had labored in the past. They preferred to move out on their own. Since few could afford to purchase land or even rent farm acreage, they engaged in various kinds of sharecropping. Despite its limitations, sharecropping offered them the potential of a higher income, capital to engage in farming, the possibility of greater rewards for hard work, and a significant amount of independence from white control.

The Goal of Owning Land

Only a few former slaves made the transition from sharecropping to landownership, but almost universally, the freedmen expressed their desire to own land. "What's de use of being free," one elderly black asked the journalist Whitelaw Reid in 1865, "if you don't own land enough to be buried in?" One white observer in postwar South Carolina asserted that former slaves had "a passion" to obtain land: they would sacrifice almost anything to obtain a few acres of their own. The Union general Rufus Saxon agreed, saying that freed slaves "have shown that they can appreciate freedom as the highest boon; [that] they will be industrious and provident with the same incitement which stimulates the industry of other men in free societies; that they understand the value of property and are eager for its acquisition, especially of land; that they can conduct their private affairs with sagacity, prudence and success."

Success, of course, was relative and had various meanings for former slaves. Some spoke of "getting ahead" or "accumulating wealth"; others accepted the teachings of black political leaders, northern missionaries, or Freedmen's Bureau officials who entreated them to become frugal, hard-working, and industrious; still others, after a lifetime of bondage, simply wanted to be left alone. By owning a few acres of land, planting vegetables and corn, raising a few head of livestock, hunting and fishing, they could distance themselves not only from the impersonal forces of the market place, but from their former masters as well. This was especially the case in the Sea Islands of South Carolina and Georgia, a region that has claimed the attention of scholars far out of proportion to its importance. There, [historian] Eric Foner has suggested, a unique combination of circumstances, including initial government programs, the breakup of the great plantations, black political power, and the collapse of rice production, allowed a majority of blacks to become landowners. Although access to the land made low-country freedmen ("peasants," as Foner calls them) independent and autonomous, they suffered from the same "debilitating disadvantages that afflicted peasant agriculture throughout the world, among them a credit system that made direct access to capital impossible, an inability to invest in fertilizer or machinery, vulnerability to the vagaries of the national and international markets, and the demands for taxation of an oppressive state." In short, black landowners had not risen above the barest subsistence level.

In other regions of the rural South, and in towns and cities, some blacks acquired holdings worth more than a few subsistence acres. Within five years after emancipation, the 1870 census indicates, rural blacks in the western sections of the upper South and some freedmen who migrated to urban areas in the upper and lower South already had made significant advances in accumulating property. Their success depended both on the willingness of whites not to stand in the way of their purchasing land or city property and on favorable economic circumstances. In Kentucky, Tennessee, and Missouri, some former slaves moved with little difficulty from bondage to farm ownership. With the support, and in some sections the protection, of whites, and aided by a strong demand for laborers and farm hands, the number of black rural landholders in these three states increased by 744 percent (from 775 to 6,538) during the 1860s. Some of them were only part-time farmers who also worked as day laborers, harvest hands, wood-cutters, and rail-splitters. In Boyle County, Kentucky, for exam-ple, Charles Christopher, James Warren, Harrison Bruce, and Jesse Jones, who each farmed several acres, were listed as laborers. In Pike County, Missouri, Thornton Washington, Ned Holloway, and Frederick Ball each owned between $800 and $1,000 worth of farm land, but the first two were listed in the census as hired hands, and the third as a blacksmith. Although the average hold-ings of these rural realty owners in the western states remained small—between $580 in Kentucky and $709 in Tennessee—the rise in their numbers actually kept pace with the eightfold increase in the number of free rural black families in the wake of emanci-pation. By 1870, one of twelve black rural family heads in Mis-souri, one of fifteen in Kentucky, and one of twenty-two in Ten-nessee, was a real estate owner.

The Urban Economy Grew

There was also a sharp increase in the number of urban property owners during the 1860s. In the towns and cities of the upper South, the number of black realty owners rose significantly: in Bal-timore, from 169 in 1860 to approximately 435 in 1870; in the District of Columbia, from 497 to 1,019; in Lexington, from 44 to 671; and in Wilmington, North Carolina, from 42 to 408. Repre-senting only 15 percent of the upper South's black population (266,188 of 1,808,655), city dwellers in 1870 comprised 34 per-cent of the realty owners and controlled 49 percent of the total black wealth ($8,863,500 of $18,197,400). In the District of Columbia in 1870, one out of eight black family heads owned real estate. Its value exceeded $2,305,900, or $2,263 per realty holder. This did not compare favorably with the figures for whites, who made up 68 percent of the city's population but owned 98 percent of the property. Yet the total realty holdings among urban blacks in the upper South had nearly quadrupled (from $2,285,900) in only ten years. In Wilmington, the 42 free blacks listed for 1860 owned $55,600 worth of land; the 408 black realty owners who lived there a decade later controlled holdings valued at $247,900. In Nashville, Tennessee, there were 44 antebellum black landowners, with property worth $119,400; in 1870, 65 black owners controlled $245,300. In St. Louis, 94 black real estate owners controlled $428,600 before the war; afterwards, approximately 128 owners controlled $765,100 worth of property.

Except in Charleston and New Orleans, similar growth occurred in the urban lower South. The rising demand for skilled and unskilled black workers, especially to rebuild buildings destroyed during the war, and the continued importance of small towns as trading and merchandising centers gave some freedmen an opportunity to improve their economic condition. In Selma and Mobile, Alabama; Pensacola, Florida; Savannah, Valdosta, and Augusta, Georgia; Columbia, South Carolina; and other small towns and cities in the region, the number of propertied blacks rose from 276 in 1860 to 3,366 a decade later, and their total real estate holdings jumped from $415,300 to $2,705,400. In Charleston and New Orleans, rising taxes, competition from whites for skilled jobs, and racial violence—including a major riot in the Crescent City—resulted in a drop in black wealth during the war decade: in Charleston, from $808,300 to $507,100 (or from $2,479 to $2,234 per realty owner); in New Orleans, from $2,521,300 to $2,087,100 (or $4,739 to $2,899 on average). Despite these setbacks, urban blacks in the lower South generally improved their economic position. During a decade that saw real estate values in the South drop by 45 percent, urban blacks in the lower South increased the value of their holdings from $3,744,900 to $5,299,600, an improvement of 42 percent. By 1870, one of nine urban blacks in the region owned an average of $1,229 worth of real estate.

A far greater expansion of black property ownership appears when personal as well as real property is considered. Between 1860 and 1870, the number of blacks who owned at least enough personal possessions—horses, mules, cows, wagons, plows, machinery, tools, furniture, carts, carriages—to bring their total assets above $100 grew by 947 percent, from 16,044 to 168,034. This total represented nearly one out of five black families in the South. Unlike realty owners, who were proportionately more numerous in the upper South and a few scattered areas of the Deep South, these owners of modest amounts of personal property were most numerous in the heart of the lower South—Georgia, Alabama, and Mississippi. Some former bondsmen had preserved the small personal holdings they had acquired in slavery, but most simply found it easier to buy livestock and tools than to purchase a plot of ground. Mississippi and Georgia, the two lower South states with the largest antebellum slave populations (and two of the smallest free-black populations), led all states in the total number of black property owners—Mississippi with 23,665, Georgia with 17,739. The contrast with the antebellum period also appears in the fact that 94 percent of the 1870 property owners were men (compared with 81 percent in 1860), 87 percent lived in rural areas (compared with 66 percent), 84 percent were listed as black rather than mulatto (compared with 53 percent), and 84 percent were illiterate or semiliterate (compared with 45 percent). In view of the fact that southern whites were 3.5 times more likely to own some property

Black Property Owners in the Lower South

State	Estimated Total Property Holdings		Average Property Holdings Per Owner		No. of Owners	
	1860	1870	1860	1870	1860	1870
Alabama	$ 468,300	$ 5,060,300	$2,072	$330	226	15,317
Arkansas	4,500	2,419,400	1,125	340	4	7,113
Florida	168,400	1,052,100	1,604	317	105	3,315
Georgia	256,200	5,237,000	896	295	286	17,739
Louisiana	8,159,300	7,530,200	3,674	517	2,221	14,569
Mississippi	210,500	8,248,100	3,972	349	53	23,665
South Carolina	1,895,200	4,628,700	1,760	421	1,077	10,997
Texas	53,800	3,049,800	1,681	243	32	12,535
Totals	$11,216,200	$37,225,600	$2,801	$354	4,004	105,250

and that their holdings dwarfed those of blacks, these gains may seem modest, but in relation to the property blacks owned before the Civil War the change was substantial. By 1870, blacks in the South owned $68,528,200 worth of property—an average estate of only $408, but a rise of 240 percent in a decade, and a significant step away from the destitution of slavery.

The decline in black property ownership in Charleston and New Orleans, coupled with the substantial expansion among those who controlled at least $100 worth of personal property in rural areas of the Deep South, suggests some of the economic changes occurring during the Reconstruction era among blacks who had been free before the war. The few historians who have compared the pre- and postwar condition of blacks, including Thomas Holt and David Rankin, have concentrated almost solely on the property acquisitions of black political leaders. This emphasis has tended to obscure the complex and dynamic economic transformations that were taking place among free persons of color. In the lower South free blacks, like their white neighbors, suffered from wartime destruction, the loss of slave property, and a multitude of economic problems. During the 1860s, the mean value of real estate held by black "planters" in South Carolina, Louisiana, and a few other Gulf states dropped from about $10,000 to less than $2,000, a decline nearly double the general depreciation in land values. Even those free blacks who survived the war with their estates intact—primarily urban dwellers who had invested heavily in real estate instead of in slaves—found it difficult to adjust to the rapid changes occurring in the wake of emancipation. Within a decade, most of them had passed from the scene through either death or mismanagement of their holdings.

Prewar and Postwar Land Ownership

Prewar free blacks in the upper states fared somewhat better than those in the lower South during the postwar period. Nearly one out of four free blacks who owned land in 1850 or 1860 could be found as property owners in 1870, at least as roughly gauged by the "persistence rate" in the United States population censuses. In rural areas of western states—Kentucky, Tennessee, and Missouri—where white antiproprietorship attitudes were less pronounced and the black population more widely dispersed, and in towns and cities, where there were new economic opportunities for service employment and establishing small businesses, some antebellum free blacks substantially improved their economic position during Reconstruction. Some became the most prosperous blacks in their communities—for example, Kentucky farmer Dennis Lane; Tennessee landholder Rubin Caldwell; Baltimore barber Augustus Roberts; District of Columbia restaurateur Richard Francis and hotel owner James Wormley; Alexandria, Virginia, butcher William Gray; Shelbyville, Kentucky, merchant Thomas Ballard; and St. Louis steward James Young. Others, like the Baltimore shoemaker George Adams, advanced from owning small amounts of personal property to real estate ownership. Still others entered the property-holding group for the first time.

Even with these shifts, the vast majority of postwar black property owners were former slaves. Among the 43,268 black landowners in the South in 1870, only about 2,300 had been property owners in 1850 or 1860; among the 168,034 blacks who owned at least $100 worth of real or personal property in 1870, fewer than 4,000 had been in the same class before the war. Only estimates can be made of the number of propertyless free blacks who entered the property-owning group for the first time after the war, but even if their numbers were twice as great as the number of prewar owners, by 1870 at least 84 percent of the black landowners and fully 94 percent of all black property owners had recently emerged from slavery.

Statistical evidence, of course, may be viewed from many perspectives, and it tends to minimize the human dimensions of historical change. Yet by turning attention away from political failures, market systems, and labor repression, and by focusing on the statistics of the "temporal and spatial differences" in the upper and lower South, before, during, and after the war, one can better understand the aspirations and achievements of freedmen in their first half-generation of freedom. One also can understand more fully the complex and dynamic dimensions of black economic reconstruction in the South. It is remarkable that despite regional variations, such significant numbers of freedmen became property owners during this brief period. Some acquired homes and small farms, symbols of their movement away from the past. It was a slow, tedious process, often requiring many years. Such was the case for the illiterate North Carolina black Isaac Forbes, who saved his extra earnings for more than a decade before purchasing his first farm. On December 14, 1872, at the age of fifty, Forbes put his mark on an "Indenture" between himself and Francis T. and Hanna G. Hawks:

> Witnesseth That said Hawks & wife for & in consideration of Five thousand dollars to them in hand paid by the said Forbes, have granted bargained & sold and by these presents do grant bargain & sell unto the said Isaac Forbes, his heirs & assignees, a body of land lying on Brices Creek in Craven County, bounded by the Creek on the west, by Boleyns Swamp on the south, by the lands of Henry R. Bryan on the North, and by the lands of G Moye & others on the east, being the entire body of lands owned by the late Judge Gaston on the north side of Boleyns Swamp, containing twelve hundred acres more or less, To have & to hold the said lands with all privileges and appurtenances thereunto belonging to him the said Isaac his heirs, and assignees forever.

How Forbes acquired such a large amount of money is not known, but his sense of accomplishment and triumph must have been substantial, and it undoubtedly was shared by other former slaves who struggled to move beyond the suffering and degradation of perpetual bondage.

Viewpoint 8

"Few whites, Northern or Southern, ever fully accepted the idea of racial equality with former slaves."

Reconstruction Did Not Improve the Economic or Political Status of Southern Blacks

Chester J. Wynne

In the following viewpoint Reconstruction scholar Chester J. Wynne argues that the abolition of slavery did not end discrimination against African Americans. According to Wynne, southern legislatures passed laws that limited employment opportunities for blacks. Although many of these laws, known as Black Codes, were eventually invalidated, former slaves found it difficult to fully participate in southern society. For example, white southerners used intimidation, violence, and manipulation of voting laws to ensure that blacks could not procure political

power. Wynne concludes that blacks during Reconstruction
were forced to live under a caste system.

The end of slavery might have destroyed the social system of
the Old South, but it did nothing to eliminate racism. As early
as 1865 legislatures in all Southern states except North Carolina
enacted Black Codes designed to control blacks and to restrict
their civil rights. Although these regulations varied from state to
state, the most common provisions included the establishment of
racial segregation in public places, the prohibition of interracial
marriage, and the legal recognition of marriages between blacks.
Black Codes also prevented blacks from serving on juries or from
testifying against whites in court, though they could give testimony against other blacks. In some states, such as Mississippi,
these laws reinstituted many of the criminal provisions of the slave
codes. The Mississippi law, for example, declared that "all penal
and criminal laws now in force describing the mode of punishment of crimes and misdemeanors committed by slaves, free negroes, or mulattoes are hereby reenacted, and decreed to be in full
force against all freedmen, free negroes, and mulattoes."

Limits on Employment

The Black Codes in general forbade blacks from entering any but
agricultural employment. In Mississippi they prevented blacks
from buying or renting farmland and required them to sign an an-
nual labor contract with a white employer; in South Carolina they
made it illegal for blacks to purchase or own city lots and compelled them to pay a tax of between $10 and $100 to enter an occupation other than farming or domestic service. Blacks were also
prohibited from leaving the plantation, or from entertaining guests
upon it, without permission. If blacks could not give evidence of
being employed, they could be detained under a charge of vagrancy
and fined, or bound to work for a white landowner if unable to
pay. The vagrancy statute imposed involuntary labor as punishment for a wide array of persons deemed antisocial, including:

rogues and vagabonds, idle and dissipated persons, beggars,

jugglers, or persons practicing unlawful games or plays, run-aways, common drunkards, common night-walkers, lewd, wanton, or lascivious persons, . . . common railers and brawlers, persons who neglect their calling or employment, misspend what they earn, or do not provide for the support of themselves or their families, or dependents, and all other idle and disorderly persons, including all who neglect all lawful business, habitually misspend their time by frequenting houses of ill-fame, gaming houses, or tippling shops.

Apprenticeship laws authorized the state to bind out to white employers black children whose parents could not support them or who were "not teaching them habits of industry and honesty; or are persons of notoriously bad character."

Although either the Federal Army, the Freedmen's Bureau, or the Civil Rights Act (1866) invalidated most of the Black Codes, these laws reveal what the contours of social and race relations in the post–Civil War South would have been if left entirely in the hands of whites. As African American historian W.E.B. Du Bois observed, the Black Codes represented "what the South proposed to do to the emancipated Negro, unless restrained by the nation." Black Congressman Josiah Walls warned that the Black Codes indicated what Southern Democrats would do "if they should ever again obtain control of this Government." In essence, whites intended these laws to keep blacks a propertyless, rural, laboring class, slaves in everything but name.

A Weakened Position

With the adoption of the Black Codes, the freedmen, indeed, found themselves cruelly thrust back into much the same position they had occupied as slaves. The laws that had recognized their citizenship and their rights disappeared. Some freedmen nonetheless protested their mistreatment. A letter to the governor of Mississippi from a group of freedmen asked that if "Mississippi has abolished slavery, . . . does she mean it or is it a policy for the present?" Further, they pointed out that "now we are free, we do not want to be hunted by negro runners and their hounds unless we are guilty of a criminal crime."

Most blacks sensibly realized that their protests would have little effect on the situation and might in some ways even make it worse. A writer in one African American newspaper declared that the Black Codes "express an average of the justice and humanity which the late slaveholders possess." He felt assured, though, that with the aid of the federal government "the right will prevail and truth [will] triumph in the end." For the time being, the government appeared to respond sympathetically to the plight of blacks, suspending the Black Codes in several states. Some Southern state legislatures repealed the harshest laws on their own. While the Codes were thought "dead," however, the forces that had created them were very much alive.

With the failure of the Black Codes, Southern whites tried to curb the freedom and power of blacks through intimidation, violence, and terror, with the largest number of violent acts arising from the attempts of blacks to assert their rights. Freedmen were assaulted and, in some cases, murdered for not satisfying their employers, for trying to buy or rent land, or for simply trying to leave the plantations on which they had once been enslaved. One Tennessee newspaper reported that white "regulators" were "riding about whipping, maiming and killing all the negroes who do not obey the orders of their former masters, just as if slavery existed." Many former black soldiers who had fought for the Union returned home only to find cinders and ashes. The rising tide of racist violence prompted one Louisiana freedman to declare: "I would say to every colored soldier, 'Bring your gun home'." Other blacks wearily realized that out of the ruin of the Civil War another conflict was smoldering. Whites knew it, too, for a former governor of North Carolina remarked "with reference to Emancipation, we are at the beginning of the war."

The Rise of the Klan

Perhaps the greatest threat to the freedmen was the appearance of a new organization determined to unnerve and overpower blacks and their white supporters: the Ku Klux Klan. Organized in 1866 in Pulaski, Tennessee, the Klan set out to restore white supremacy throughout the South. Klansmen rode about the Southern countryside wearing white masks and robes, issuing threats, harassing blacks, and on occasion engaging in destruction, violence, and murder. During their brief career, the Klan and similar groups such as the Knights of the White Camellia and the White League "whipped, shot, hanged, robbed, raped, and otherwise outraged Negroes and Republicans across the South in the name of preserving white civilization."

Congress struck back at the Klan with three Enforcement Acts passed in 1870 and 1871. The first of these measures made it a federal offense to interfere with any citizen's right to vote. The second placed the election of Congressmen under the supervision of federal election officials and marshals. The third, the so-called Ku Klux Klan Act, made it illegal to engage in conspiracies, to wear disguises in public, and to resist, threaten, or in any way intimidate officials of the courts or the government.

Federal mandates and prosecutions weakened the Klan, but such societies as the Mississippi Rifle Club and the South Carolina Red Shirts continued to harass blacks and white Republicans, enabling conservative whites gradually to reassume control of government and society in one Southern state after another. Republicans fell out of power in Virginia and Tennessee in 1869 and Georgia and North Carolina in 1870, even though the "Old North State" had a Republican governor until 1876. Republicans held on longer in the states of the Deep South, which had larger black populations than those in the upper South. In the elections of 1876, however, voters dismissed the Republicans from office in South Carolina, Louisiana, and Florida, the three remaining states where they held sway.

Why Attitudes Changed

Northern support for Reconstruction (1865–1877) had begun to wane with the Panic of 1873. Economic hard times distracted Northerners from the problems of the former slaves and made Reconstruction programs seem an expensive luxury. Even whites who favored racial equality usually thought in terms of legal equality, which they believed would naturally follow from emancipation. Yet, for freedom to be meaningful and equality assured, the federal government had to guarantee the physical safety of black men and women and support their liberty by giving them land.

When the government failed to do so, Reconstruction faltered and then collapsed.

For a brief period during the 1870s and 1880s greater flexibility and tolerance had characterized race relations in the South. The former slave owner, wrote a South Carolina newspaper editor, "has no desire to browbeat, maltreat, and spit upon the colored man." There lingered among many white Southerners feelings of benevolence and paternalism toward blacks, and in any event most did not regard blacks as a threat to the existing social and political order.

Such attitudes began to change in the early 1890s when the Populist, or People's, Party tried to organize black and white farmers into a political coalition to challenge for control of state governments throughout the South. "You are kept apart," Populist leader Tom Watson of Georgia told an audience of black and white farmers, "in order that you may be separately fleeced." Such language frightened those in power. They responded by appealing to the fears of Southern whites that the South would again come under "Negro domination," as they believed had been the case during Reconstruction.

Manipulating Elections

Since competition for the black vote was growing, that relatively small group of men who dominated Southern politics at the end of the nineteenth century, known as the Bourbons, reasoned it was best to eliminate the black vote altogether. The Bourbons were members of the Democratic Party. As long as they could manipulate the black vote to their liking, they had no objection to blacks' going to the polls and selecting the Democratic candidate of their choice. It was, however, another matter entirely when their Republican, Independent, and especially Populist adversaries began striving to capture the black vote. Under those circumstances, the right of blacks to vote had to be withdrawn.

The Fifteenth Amendment (1870) made it impossible simply to disfranchise blacks, so the Bourbons devised other, less direct, means to keep them from voting. They instituted a poll tax that most blacks could not afford to pay and literacy tests that most blacks, and many whites, could not pass.

Mississippi led the way in the disfranchisement of blacks. At a state convention held in 1890, delegates modified the Reconstruction constitution of 1868, which had extended suffrage to blacks. First, Mississippi established a new residency requirement of two years in the state and one year in the election district that often prevented both black and white tenant farmers, who habitually moved every year, from voting. Second, the new provisions disqualified voters convicted of certain crimes such as vagrancy, to which blacks were uncommonly susceptible. Third, the reforms mandated that all taxes, including the poll tax, be paid by 1 February of election year. Even those rare blacks who could afford to pay their taxes either moved frequently or were not in the habit of keeping careful records. They had plenty of time to lose tax receipts before election day arrived in the fall and were thus barred from voting. Fourth, the new regulations instituted a literacy test. To assist illiterate whites who could not, for example, read a passage from the Constitution, most Southern states instituted what became known as the "understanding clause." An election official read a portion of the Constitution to a potential white voter and then asked if he had understood it. If he answered "yes," he was permitted to vote.

Other states found different ways for whites to get around the literacy requirement. In 1895 the South Carolina legislature declared that owning property assessed at $300 qualified an illiterate voter. Many more whites than blacks met the prerequisite. Three years later the Louisiana state legislature invented the ingenious "grandfather clause," which enabled illiterates to vote if their fathers or grandfathers had been eligible on 1 January 1867, when all blacks in the state had been disfranchised. By 1910 the legislatures of Oklahoma, Alabama, Georgia, North Carolina, and Virginia had incorporated the grandfather clause into state election laws. Such restrictions were effective in limiting the black vote. In 1896, for example, 130,000 blacks registered to vote in Louisiana; by 1900 that number had fallen to 5,320. According to the census of 1900, Alabama had 121,259 literate black men over the age of twenty-one, all of whom ought to have been eligible to vote; only 3,742 were registered.

The federal government did little to rectify the situation. In 1890 the Senate, apparently not wishing to interfere in the internal affairs of the states, defeated a bill sponsored by Representative Henry Cabot Lodge (R.-Mass.) that would have authorized federal supervision of state elections to reexamine the qualifications of those excluded from voting. Lodge's bill marked the last significant attempt to protect black voters until Congress passed the Voting Rights Act (1965).

The Status of Civil Rights

Despite their political limitations, blacks won a few major, if short-lived, victories, chief among them passage of the Civil Rights Act (1875). Although poorly enforced, the Act outlawed discrimination in transportation, theaters, restaurants, hotels, and other places of public accommodation. In 1883, however, the U.S. Supreme Court ruled, with only one dissent, that the Fourteenth Amendment (1868) prohibited state governments from discriminating on the basis of race but did not restrict private organizations, companies, or individuals from doing so. Hence, railroad and street-car companies, restaurants, hotels, theaters, private clubs, hospitals, and the like could legally keep blacks out if they wished.

The repeal of the Civil Rights Act of 1875 did not immediately rob blacks of their rights any more than its passage had guaranteed them. In 1885, for instance, blacks in South Carolina continued to ride in first-class railway cars apparently without exciting comment. As early as 1881, by contrast, the Tennessee state legislature had required railroads operating in the state to provide separate first-class cars for blacks and whites. Not until 1888 did Mississippi require separate railway cars for blacks and whites. When in 1890 Louisiana also established separate cars for blacks and whites, Homer Plessy, an octoroon (one-eighth black) convicted for refusing to leave an all-white car, challenged the constitutionality of the law in the U.S. Supreme Court.

The justices rendered their decision in the case of *Plessy v. Ferguson* in 1896, upholding state laws that mandated segregation. Writing the majority opinion, Justice Henry Brown Billings from Massachusetts declared that segregation laws "have been generally, if not universally, recognized as within the competency of state legislatures in the exercise of their police power." Separate seating arrangements, the majority of the Court concluded, thus did not deprive blacks of their constitutional rights. The sole dissenting voice came from Justice John Marshall Harlan, a former slaveholder and Unionist from Kentucky, who had also opposed repeal of the Civil Rights Act of 1875. "In my opinion," Harlan wrote, "the judgment this day rendered will, in time, prove to be quite as pernicious as the decision made by this tribunal in the Dred Scott Case." The ruling, Harlan predicted, would "stimulate aggressions, more or less brutal, upon the admitted rights of colored citizens."

Events made Harlan's words prophetic. Soon the principle of segregation extended to every aspect of life for blacks, from public accommodations to recreation and sports to health care and employment. The violence that Justice Harlan had foretold also became a reality. Between 1890 and 1899 the number of lynchings that occurred in the United States averaged 187.5 per year, 82 percent of which took place in the South. In 1892 black journalist and social activist Ida B. Wells launched what eventually became an international movement opposed to lynching when she wrote a series of articles about the lynching of three friends in Memphis, Tennessee. The antilynching movement attracted considerable support in all regions of the United States, including the South, much of it coming from white women. Wells's goal was the enactment of a federal antilynching law, which would empower the U.S. government to prosecute those responsible for lynchings when local and state governments failed or refused to do so.

The opposition to lynching, however, was an exception to the general support for white supremacy. Few whites, Northern or Southern, ever fully accepted the idea of racial equality with former slaves. In time, Northerners who feared the invasion of blacks into their states became increasingly sympathetic to the view of Southerners that black equality really meant the oppression of white people. The reality that blacks faced in both the North and the South during the last thirty years of the nineteenth century was the emergence of a racial caste system embodied in the laws of the United States and sustained by the attitudes and conduct of whites. Regrettably, the hopes that the majority of black Americans had long entertained for equality and integration remained unfulfilled.

CHAPTER 4

Historians Debate Reconstruction

Chapter Preface

By most historical accounts, Reconstruction formally ended on March 3, 1877, the day that Rutherford B. Hayes was inaugurated president. His inauguration followed months of political wrangling that culminated in what became known as the Compromise of 1877. Under that compromise the Democrats agreed to let Republican candidate Hayes receive twenty disputed electoral votes, thereby awarding him the presidency. In exchange, they demanded the withdrawal of all remaining federal troops from the South and the end of federal interference in southern state governments.

Although Reconstruction was not solely about civil rights, the rapid decline in blacks' civil rights in the two decades that followed the Compromise of 1877 helps explain why many scholars believe Reconstruction was a failure. For example, as northern citizens became engrossed with issues such as the sharp influx of immigrants, the growth of the labor movement, and the conquest of the West, they began to lose interest in the fate of southern blacks. Economics was a particular concern. Eighteen thousand businesses failed and 3 million jobs were lost during the five-year depression brought upon by the Panic of 1873, which had been caused by the collapse of the banking house of Jay Cooke and Company. These events drew the public's attention away from Reconstruction and helped pave the way to its end. However, it would be two major Supreme Court rulings—an 1883 decision on the Civil Rights Act of 1875, and 1896's seminal *Plessy v. Ferguson*—that would definitively close the books on Reconstruction and simultaneously negate many of that era's achievements.

In February 1875 Congress had passed a civil rights bill that prohibited discrimination in hotels, restaurants, theaters, and public transportation. However, the bill did not greatly change southern society during its eight-year history. In *Reconstruction: After the Civil War*, John Hope Franklin writes, "The Civil Rights Act of 1875 was a dead letter from the day of its enactment, and Southerners boasted that it was not being enforced and could not be enforced anywhere in the South."

In 1883 the Supreme Court heard several suits alleging that blacks had been denied accommodations and privileges at inns, theaters, and rail cars throughout the nation, in violation of the Civil Rights Act of 1875. The majority decision, written by Justice Joseph P. Bradley, voided the first two sections of the act and stated that the act was unconstitutional because Congress did not have authority over private individual rights in public places. According to the Court the only lawful section of the act was the one that required the inclusion of blacks in jury pools. In the decision Bradley explained how the act did not meet the standards set by the Thirteenth or Fourteenth Amendments, which ended slavery and guaranteed all Americans equal protection of the laws. Bradley asserted that refusing to accommodate someone in a theater or on a train "has nothing to do with slavery or involuntary servitude, and that if it is violative of any right of the party, his redress is to be sought under the laws of the State." He also maintained, "[The Fourteenth Amendment] does not invest Congress with power to legislate upon subjects which are within the domain of state legislation; but to provide modes of redress against the operation of state laws."

Thirteen years later, the Court heard arguments in the case of *Plessy v. Ferguson*. In 1890 the Louisiana legislature had passed a statute requiring "that all railway companies carrying passengers in their coaches in this state shall provide equal but separate accommodations for the white and colored races." The penalty for sitting in the wrong compartment was a twenty-five dollar fine or twenty days in jail. On June 7, 1892, Homer Plessy, who was seven-eighths white and one-eighth black, was jailed for sitting in the "white" car of the Eastern Louisiana Railroad. Plessy argued that the Louisiana law violated the Thirteenth and Fourteenth Amendments, and his case eventually reached the Supreme Court.

The Court issued its decision, written by Justice Henry Billings Brown, on May 18, 1896. By a 7-1 vote (Justice John Marshall Harlan cast the lone dissenting vote and another justice sat out the case) the Supreme Court ruled that "separate but equal" accommodations were constitutional under the Fourteenth Amendment's equal protection clause. Brown also asserted that the statute did not violate the Thirteenth Amendment: "A statute which implies merely a legal distinction between the white and colored races . . . has no tendency to destroy the legal equality of the two races, or re-establish a state of involuntary servitude." The Court's support of "separate but equal" led to the inception of other laws, known as Jim Crow laws, that further institutionalized segregation. *Plessy v. Ferguson* would stand until 1954, when the Supreme Court ruled in favor of integration in its *Brown v. Board of Education* decision.

The Supreme Court's decisions in the 1883 and 1896 cases reflected the predominant attitude toward blacks and their fight for equality in the final years of the nineteenth century. As Robert Cruden explains in *The Negro in Reconstruction*, "For a generation after 1876 black men voted, held public office, and sat in Congress—but in ever diminishing numbers and on terms reflecting an understanding between such blacks and Southern Conservatives. For a time there was some respect for black civil rights. What remained of those, as well as of black political rights, were consumed in the flames of the political warfare of the 90's."

The Reconstruction era ended because of the animosity of southern whites toward blacks and the indifference of northern whites toward the plight of black Americans. It would not be until the 1950s that a second "Reconstruction"—the civil rights movement—would reshape the American social and political landscape, making it possible to finally guarantee equal rights to black Americans. The twelve-year period known as Reconstruction, during which so much hope flourished, in the end left black Americans feeling like second-class citizens. The authors in this chapter evaluate the immediate and long-term effects of Reconstruction on black Americans and the nation.

Viewpoint 1

"For blacks [Reconstruction's] failure was a disaster whose magnitude cannot be obscured by the genuine accomplishments that did endure."

Reconstruction Was a Failure

Eric Foner

In the following viewpoint Eric Foner argues that Reconstruction failed to improve the political and economic status of African Americans. According to Foner, this failure can be attributed to Southern racism, violence throughout the South, and the lack of resolve among northern politicians. He adds that although Reconstruction was unsuccessful, historians in the early twentieth century were wrong to assert that the failure was caused by the decision to give blacks political power. Foner is a professor of history at Columbia University and the author of numerous books, including *Reconstruction: America's Unfinished Revolution, 1863–1877*, from which this viewpoint has been excerpted.

In the words of W.E.B. Du Bois, "the slave went free; stood a brief moment in the sun; then moved back again toward slav-

Eric Foner, *Reconstruction: America's Unfinished Revolution, 1863–1877*. New York: Harper & Row, 1988. Copyright © 1988 by Eric Foner. Reproduced by permission.

ery." The magnitude of the Redeemer counterrevolution[1] underscored both the scope of the transformation Reconstruction had assayed and the consequences of its failure. To be sure, the era of emancipation and Republican rule did not lack enduring accomplishments. The tide of change rose and then receded, but it left behind an altered landscape. The freedmen's political and civil equality proved transitory, but the autonomous black family and a network of religious and social institutions survived the end of Reconstruction. Nor could the seeds of educational progress planted then be entirely uprooted. While wholly inadequate for pupils of both races, schooling under the Redeemers represented a distinct advance over the days when blacks were excluded altogether from a share in public services.

If blacks failed to achieve the economic independence envisioned in the aftermath of the Civil War, Reconstruction closed off even more oppressive alternatives than the Redeemers' New South. The post-Reconstruction labor system embodied neither a return to the closely supervised gang labor of antebellum days, nor the complete dispossession and immobilization of the black labor force and coercive apprenticeship systems envisioned by white Southerners in 1865 and 1866. Nor were blacks, as in twentieth-century South Africa, barred from citizenship, herded into labor reserves, or prohibited by law from moving from one part of the country to another. As illustrated by the small but growing number of black landowners, businessmen, and professionals, the doors of economic opportunity that had opened could never be completely closed. Without Reconstruction, moreover, it is difficult to imagine the establishment of a framework of legal rights enshrined in the Constitution that, while flagrantly violated after 1877, created a vehicle for future federal intervention in Southern affairs. As a result of this unprecedented redefinition of the American body politic, the South's racial system remained regional rather than national, an outcome of great importance when economic opportunities at last opened in the North.

Nonetheless, whether measured by the dreams inspired by

1. Redeemers were white southern Democrats who returned to power at the end of Reconstruction.

emancipation or the more limited goals of securing blacks' rights as citizens and free laborers, and establishing an enduring Republican presence in the South, Reconstruction can only be judged a failure. Among the host of explanations for this outcome, a few seem especially significant. Events far beyond the control of Southern Republicans—the nature of the national credit and banking systems, the depression of the 1870s, the stagnation of world demand for cotton—severely limited the prospects for far-reaching economic change. The early rejection of federally sponsored land reform left in place a planter class far weaker and less affluent than before the war, but still able to bring its prestige and experience to bear against Reconstruction. Factionalism and corruption, although hardly confined to Southern Republicans, undermined their claim to legitimacy and made it difficult for them to respond effectively to attacks by resolute opponents. The failure to develop an effective long-term appeal to white voters made it increasingly difficult for Republicans to combat the racial politics of the Redeemers. None of these factors, however, would have proved decisive without the campaign of violence that turned the electoral tide in many parts of the South, and the weakening of Northern resolve, itself a consequence of social and political changes that undermined the free labor and egalitarian precepts at the heart of Reconstruction policy.

For historians, hindsight can be a treacherous ally. Enabling us to trace the hidden patterns of past events, it beguiles us with the mirage of inevitability, the assumption that different outcomes lay beyond the limits of the possible. Certainly, the history of other plantation societies offers little reason for optimism that emancipation could have given rise to a prosperous, egalitarian South, or even one that escaped a pattern of colonial underdevelopment. Nor do the prospects for the expansion of scalawag [Southern Republican] support—essential for Southern Republicanism's long-term survival—appear in retrospect to have been anything but bleak. Outside the mountains and other enclaves of wartime Unionism, the Civil War generation of white Southerners was always likely to view the Republican party as an alien embodiment of wartime defeat and black equality. And the nation lacked not simply the will but the modern bureaucratic machinery to oversee Southern affairs in any permanent way. Perhaps the remarkable thing about Reconstruction was not that it failed, but that it was attempted at all and survived as long as it did. Yet one can, I think, imagine alternative scenarios and modest successes: the Republican party establishing itself as a permanent fixture on the Southern landscape, the North summoning the resolve to insist that the Constitution must be respected. As the experiences of Readjuster Virginia[2] and Populist-Republican North Carolina suggest, even Redemption did not entirely foreclose the possibility of biracial politics, thus raising the question of how Southern life might have been affected had Deep South blacks enjoyed genuine political freedoms when the Populist movement swept the white counties in the 1890s.

Here, however, we enter the realm of the purely speculative. What remains certain is that Reconstruction failed, and that for blacks its failure was a disaster whose magnitude cannot be obscured by the genuine accomplishments that did endure. For the nation as a whole, the collapse of Reconstruction was a tragedy that deeply affected the course of its future development. If racism contributed to the undoing of Reconstruction, by the same token Reconstruction's demise and the emergence of blacks as a disenfranchised class of dependent laborers greatly facilitated racism's further spread, until by the early twentieth century it had become more deeply embedded in the nation's culture and politics than at any time since the beginning of the antislavery crusade and perhaps in our entire history. The removal of a significant portion of the nation's laboring population from public life shifted the center of gravity of American politics to the right, complicating the tasks of reformers for generations to come. Long into the twentieth century, the South remained a one-party region under the control of a reactionary ruling elite who used the same violence and fraud that had helped defeat Reconstruction to stifle internal dissent. An enduring consequence of Reconstruction's failure, the Solid South helped define the contours of American politics and weaken the prospects not simply of change in racial matters but of progressive legislation in many other realms. . . .

2. a political movement that proposed repudiating part of the state debt

Rewriting Reconstruction

By the turn of the century, as soldiers from North and South joined to take up the "white man's burden" in the Spanish-American War, Reconstruction was widely viewed as little more than a regrettable detour on the road to reunion. To the bulk of the white South, it had become axiomatic that Reconstruction had been a time of "savage tyranny" that "accomplished not one useful result, and left behind it, not one pleasant recollection." Black suffrage, wrote Joseph Le Conte, who had fled South Carolina for a professorship at the University of California to avoid teaching black students, was now seen by "all thoughtful men" as "the greatest political crime ever perpetrated by any people." In more sober language, many Northerners, including surviving architects of Congressional policy, concurred in these judgments. "Years of thinking and observation" had convinced O.O. Howard "that the restoration of their lands to the planters provided for [a] future better for the negroes." John Sherman's recollections recorded a similar change of heart: "After this long lapse of time I am convinced that Mr. Johnson's [President Andrew Johnson] scheme of reorganization was wise and judicious. . . . It is unfortunate that it had not the sanction of Congress."

This rewriting of Reconstruction's history was accorded scholarly legitimacy—to its everlasting shame—by the nation's fraternity of professional historians. Early in the twentieth century a group of young Southern scholars gathered at Columbia University to study the Reconstruction era under the guidance of Professors John W. Burgess and William A. Dunning. Blacks, their mentors taught, were "children" utterly incapable of appreciating the freedom that had been thrust upon them. The North did "a monstrous thing" in granting them suffrage, for "a black skin means membership in a race of men which has never of itself succeeded in subjecting passion to reason, has never, therefore, created any civilization of any kind." No political order could survive in the South unless founded on the principle of racial inequality. The students' works on individual Southern states echoed these sentiments. Reconstruction, concluded the study of North Carolina, was an attempt by "selfish politicians, backed by the federal government . . . to Africanize the State and deprive the people through misrule and oppression of most that life held dear." The views of the Dunning School shaped historical writing for generations, and achieved wide popularity through D.W. Griffith's film *Birth of a Nation* (which glorified the Ku Klux Klan and had its premiere at the White House during Woodrow Wilson's Presidency), James Ford Rhodes's popular multivolume chronicle of the Civil War era, and the national best-seller *The Tragic Era* by Claude G. Bowers. Southern whites, wrote Bowers, "literally were put to the torture" by "emissaries of hate" who inflamed "the negroes' egotism" and even inspired "lustful assaults" by blacks upon white womanhood.

Few interpretations of history have had such far-reaching consequences as this image of Reconstruction. As Francis B. Simkins, a South Carolina–born historian, noted during the 1930s, "the alleged horrors of Reconstruction" did much to freeze the mind of the white South in unalterable opposition to outside pressures for social change and to any thought of breaching Democratic ascendancy, eliminating segregation, or restoring suffrage to disenfranchised blacks. They also justified Northern indifference to the nullification of the Fourteenth and Fifteenth Amendments. Apart from a few white dissenters like Simkins, it was left to black writers to challenge the prevailing orthodoxy. In the early years of [the twentieth century] this century, none did so more tirelessly than former Mississippi Congressman John R. Lynch, then living in Chicago, who published a series of devastating critiques of the racial biases and historical errors of Rhodes and Bowers. "I do not hesitate to assert," he wrote, "that the Southern Reconstruction Governments were the best governments those States ever had." In 1917, Lynch voiced the hope that "a fair, just, and impartial historian will, some day, write a history covering the Reconstruction period, [giving] the actual facts of what took place."

A Different Interpretation

Only in the family traditions and collective folk memories of the black community did a different version of Reconstruction survive. Growing up in the 1920s, Pauli Murray was "never allowed to forget" that she walked in "proud shoes" because her grandfather, Robert G. Fitzgerald, had "fought for freedom" in the Union

Army and then enlisted as a teacher in the "second war" against the powerlessness and ignorance inherited from slavery. When the Works Progress Administration sent agents into the black belt during the Great Depression to interview former slaves, they found Reconstruction remembered for its disappointments and betrayals, but also as a time of hope, possibility, and accomplishment. Bitterness still lingered over the federal government's failure to distribute land or protect blacks' civil and political rights. "The Yankees helped free us, so they say," declared eighty-one-year-old former slave Thomas Hall, "but they let us be put back in slavery again." Yet coupled with this disillusionment were proud, vivid recollections of a time when "the colored used to hold office." Some pulled from their shelves dusty scrapbooks of clippings from Reconstruction newspapers; others could still recount the names of local black leaders. "They made pretty fair officers," remarked one elderly freedman; "I thought them was good times in the country," said another. Younger blacks spoke of being taught by their parents "about the old times, mostly about the Reconstruction, and the Ku Klux." "I know folks think the books tell the truth, but they shore don't," one eighty-eight-year-old former slave told the WPA.

For some blacks, such memories helped to keep alive the aspirations of the Reconstruction era. "This here used to be a good county," said Arkansas freedman Boston Blackwell, "but I tell you it sure is tough now. I think it's wrong—exactly wrong that we can't vote now." "I does believe that the negro ought to be given more privileges in voting," echoed Taby Jones, born a slave in South Carolina in 1850, "because they went through the reconstruction period with banners flying." For others, Reconstruction inspired optimism that better times lay ahead. "The Bible says, 'What has been will be again'," said Alabama sharecropper Ned Cobb. Born in 1885, Cobb never cast a vote in his entire life, yet he never forgot that outsiders had once taken up the black cause—an indispensable source of hope for one conscious of his own weakness in the face of overwhelming and hostile local power. When radical Northerners ventured South in the 1930s to help organize black agricultural workers, Cobb seemed almost to have been waiting for them: "The whites came down to bring emancipation, and left before it was over. . . . Now they've come to finish the job." The legacy of Reconstruction affected the 1930s revival of black militancy in other ways as well. Two leaders of the Alabama Share Croppers Union, Ralph and Thomas Gray, claimed to be descended from a Reconstruction legislator. (Like many nineteenth-century predecessors, Ralph Gray paid with his life for challenging the South's social order—he was killed in a shootout with a posse while guarding a union meeting.)

Twenty more years elapsed before another generation of black Southerners launched the final challenge to the racial system of the New South. A few participants in the civil rights movement thought of themselves as following a path blazed after the Civil War. Discussing the reasons for his involvement, one black Mississippian spoke of the time when "a few Negroes was admitted into the government of the State of Mississippi and to the United States." Reconstruction's legacy was also evident in the actions of federal judge Frank Johnson, who fought a twelve-year battle for racial justice with Alabama Governor George Wallace. Johnson hailed from Winston County, a center of Civil War Unionism, and his great-grandfather had served as a Republican sheriff during Reconstruction. By this time, however, the Reconstruction generation had passed from the scene and even within the black community, memories of the period had all but disappeared. Yet the institutions created or consolidated after the Civil War—the black family, school, and church—provided the base from which the modern civil rights revolution sprang. And for its legal strategy, the movement returned to the laws and amendments of Reconstruction.

"The river has its bend, and the longest road must terminate." Reverend Peter Randolph, a former slave, wrote these words as the dark night of injustice settled over the South. Nearly a century elapsed before the nation again attempted to come to terms with the implications of emancipation and the political and social agenda of Reconstruction. In many ways, it has yet to do so.

Viewpoint 2

"The Negro governments in the South accomplished much of positive good."

Reconstruction Was Not a Failure

W.E.B. Du Bois

Many of the first generation of Reconstruction scholars, such as William Dunning, labeled the era a failure, placing much of the blame on the Radical Republicans who governed the postwar South. One of the first people to defend the outcome of Reconstruction was historian and civil rights activist W.E.B. Du Bois. In the following viewpoint Du Bois contends that Reconstruction should not be considered a failure. According to Du Bois blacks enjoyed far more educational and political opportunities than before the war. He also defends southern governments against charges of corruption, contending that black politicians brought lasting and beneficial changes to the region, such as democratic government, free public schools, and improved state constitutions.

There is danger to-day [1909] that between the intense feeling of the South and the conciliatory spirit of the North grave injustice will be done the Negro American in the history of Reconstruction. Those who see in Negro suffrage the cause of the main

W.E.B. Du Bois, "Reconstruction and Its Benefits," *American Historical Review*, vol. 15, July 1910, pp. 781–99.

evils of Reconstruction must remember that if there had not been a single freedman left in the South after the war the problems of Reconstruction would still have been grave. Property in slaves to the extent of perhaps two thousand million dollars had suddenly disappeared. One thousand five hundred more millions, representing the Confederate war debt, had largely disappeared. Large amounts of real estate and other property had been destroyed, industry had been disorganized, 250,000 men had been killed and many more maimed. With this went the moral effect of an unsuccessful war with all its letting down of social standards and quickening of hatred and discouragement—a situation which would make it difficult under any circumstances to reconstruct a new government and a new civilization. Add to all this the presence of four million freedmen and the situation is further complicated. . . .

Three Key Agencies

How to train and treat these ex-slaves easily became a central problem of Reconstruction, although by no means the only problem. Three agencies undertook the solution of this problem at first and their influence is apt to be forgotten. Without them the problems of Reconstruction would have been far graver than they were. These agencies were: (a) the Negro church, (b) the Negro school, and (c) the Freedmen's Bureau. After the war the white churches of the South got rid of their Negro members and the Negro church organizations of the North invaded the South. The 20,000 members of the African Methodist Episcopal Church in 1856 leaped to 75,000 in 1866 and 200,000 in 1876, while their property increased sevenfold. The Negro Baptists with 150,000 members in 1850 had fully a half million in 1870. There were, before the end of Reconstruction, perhaps 10,000 local bodies touching the majority of the freed population, centering almost the whole of their social life, and teaching them organization and autonomy. They were primitive, ill-governed, at times fantastic groups of human beings, and yet it is difficult to exaggerate the influence of this new responsibility—the first social institution fully controlled by black men in America, with traditions that rooted back to Africa and with possibilities which make the 35,000 Negro American churches to-day, with their three and one-half million members, the most powerful Negro institutions in the world.

With the Negro church, but separate from it, arose the school as the first expression of the missionary activity of Northern religious bodies. Seldom in the history of the world has an almost totally illiterate population been given the means of self-education in so short a time. The movement started with the Negroes themselves and they continued to form the dynamic force behind it. . . . The education of this mass had to begin at the top with the training of teachers, and within a few years a dozen colleges and normal schools started; by 1877, 571,506 Negro children were in school. There can be no doubt that these schools were a great conservative steadying force to which the South owes much. It must not be forgotten that among the agents of the Freedmen's Bureau were not only soldiers and politicians but school-teachers and educational leaders like Edmund Ware and Erastus Cravath. . . .

The Freedmen's Bureau was an attempt to establish a government guardianship over the Negroes and insure their economic and civil rights. Its establishment was a herculean task both physically and socially, and it not only met the solid opposition of the white South, but even the North looked at the new thing as socialistic and over-paternal. It accomplished a great task but it was repudiated. Carl Schurz in 1865 felt warranted in saying

> that not half of the labor that has been done in the south this year, or will be done there next year, would have been or would be done but for the exertions of the Freedmen's Bureau. . . . No other agency, except one placed there by the national government, could have wielded that moral power whose interposition was so necessary to prevent the southern society from falling at once into the chaos of a general collision between its different elements.

Notwithstanding this the Bureau was temporary, was regarded as a makeshift and soon abandoned.

Seeking Suffrage

Meantime, partial Negro suffrage seemed not only just but almost inevitable. [Abraham] Lincoln in 1864 "cautiously suggested" to Louisiana's private consideration, "whether some of the colored people may not be let in, as, for instance, the very intelligent, and especially those who fought gallantly in our ranks. They would probably help, in some trying to come, to keep the jewel of liberty in the family of freedom." Indeed, the "family of freedom" in Louisiana being somewhat small just then, who else was to be intrusted with the "jewel"? Later and for different reasons, [Andrew] Johnson in 1865 wrote to Mississippi:

> If you could extend the elective franchise to all persons of color who can read the Constitution of the United States in English and write their names, and to all persons of color who own real estate valued at not less than two hundred and fifty dollars, and pay taxes thereon, you would completely disarm the adversary and set an example the other States will follow. This you can do with perfect safety, and you thus place the southern States, in reference to free persons of color, upon the same basis with the free States. I hope and trust your convention will do this.

Meantime the Negroes themselves began to ask for the suffrage— the Georgia Convention in Augusta, 1866, advocating "a proposition to give those who could write and read well, and possessed a certain property qualification, the right of suffrage." The reply of the South to these suggestions was decisive. In Tennessee alone was any action attempted that even suggested possible Negro suffrage in the future, and that failed. In all other states the "Black Codes" adopted were certainly not reassuring to friends of freedom. . . .

Three Possible Courses

The United States government might now have taken any one of three courses:

1. Allowed the whites to reorganize the states and take no measures to enfranchise the freedmen.
2. Allowed the whites to reorganize the states but provided that after the lapse of a reasonable length of time there should be no discrimination in the right of suffrage on account of "race, color or previous condition of servitude."
3. Admitted all men, black and white, to take part in reorganizing the states and then provided that future restrictions on

the suffrage should be made on any basis except "race, color and previous condition of servitude."

The first course was clearly inadmissible since it meant virtually giving up the great principle on which the war was largely fought and won, *i.e.*, human freedom; a giving of freedom which contented itself with an edict, and then turned the "freed" slaves over to the tender mercies of their impoverished and angry ex-masters was no gift at all. The second course was theoretically attractive but practically impossible. It meant at least a prolongation of slavery and instead of attempts to raise the freedmen, it gave the white community strong incentives for keeping the blacks down so that as few as possible would ever qualify for the suffrage. Negro schools would have been discouraged and economic fetters would have held the black man as a serf for an indefinite time. On the other hand, the arguments for universal Negro suffrage from the start were strong and are still strong, and no one would question their strength were it not for the assumption that the experiment failed. [Famous black abolitionist] Frederick Douglass said to President Johnson: "Your noble and humane predecessor placed in our hands the sword to assist in saving the nation, and we do hope that you, his able successor, will favorably regard the placing in our hands the ballot with which to save ourselves." And when Johnson demurred on account of the hostility between blacks and poor whites, a committee of prominent colored men replied:

> Even if it were true, as you allege, that the hostility of the
> blacks toward the poor whites must necessarily project itself
> into a state of freedom, and that this enmity between the two
> races is even more intense in a state of freedom than in a state
> of slavery, in the name of Heaven, we reverently ask, how can
> you, in view of your professed desire to promote the welfare
> of the black man, deprive him of all means of defence, and
> clothe him whom you regard as his enemy in the panoply of
> political power? . . .

The steps that ended in the Fifteenth Amendment [which gave black men the right to vote] were not, however, taken suddenly. The Negroes were given the right by universal suffrage to join in reconstructing the state governments and the reasons for it were cogently set forth in the report of the Joint Committee on Reconstruction in 1866, which began as follows:

> A large proportion of the population had become, instead of mere chattels, free men and citizens. Through all the past struggle these had remained true and loyal, and had, in large numbers, fought on the side of the Union. It was impossible to abandon them without securing them their rights as free men and citizens. The whole civilized world would have cried out against such base ingratitude, and the bare idea is offensive to all right-thinking men. Hence it became important to inquire what could be done to secure their rights, civil and political.

Negro Political Power

For such reasons the Negro was enfranchised. What was the result? No language has been spared to describe these results as the worst imaginable. Nor is it necessary to dispute for a moment that there were bad results, and bad results arising from Negro suffrage; but it may be questioned if the results were as bad as painted or if Negro suffrage was the prime cause.

Let us not forget that the white South believed it to be of vital interest to its welfare that the experiment of Negro suffrage should fail ignominiously, and that almost to a man the whites were willing to insure this failure either by active force or passive acquiescence; that beside this there were, as might be expected, men, black and white, Northern and Southern, only too eager to take advantage of such a situation for feathering their own nests. The results in such case had to be evil but to charge the evil to Negro suffrage is unfair. It may be charged to anger, poverty, venality, and ignorance; but the anger and poverty were the almost inevitable aftermath of war; the venality was much greater among whites than Negroes, and while ignorance was the curse of the Negroes, the fault was not theirs, and they took the initiative to correct it.

The chief charges against the Negro governments are extravagance, theft, and incompetency of officials. There is no serious charge that these governments threatened civilization or the foundations of social order. The charge is that they threatened property, and that they were inefficient. These charges are in part undoubtedly true, but they are often exaggerated. . . .

That the Negroes led by astute thieves became tools and received a small share of the spoils is true. But two considerations must be added: much of the legislation which resulted in fraud was represented to the Negroes as good legislation, and thus their votes were secured by deliberate misrepresentation. . . .

The Accomplishments of Negro Government

Granted then that the Negroes were to some extent venal but to a much larger extent ignorant and deceived, the question is: did they show any signs of a disposition to learn better things? The theory of democratic government is not that the will of the people is always right, but rather that normal human beings of average intelligence will, if given a chance, learn the right and best course by bitter experience. This is precisely what the Negro voters showed indubitable signs of doing. First, they strove for schools to abolish ignorance, and, second, a large and growing number of them revolted against the carnival of extravagance and stealing that marred the beginning of Reconstruction, and joined with the best elements to institute reform. . . . The greatest stigma on the white South is not that it opposed Negro suffrage and resented theft and incompetence, but that when it saw the reform movement growing and even in some cases triumphing, and a larger and larger number of black voters learning to vote for honesty and ability, it still preferred a Reign of Terror to a campaign of education, and disfranchised Negroes instead of punishing rascals. . . .

In the midst of all these difficulties the Negro governments in the South accomplished much of positive good. We may recognize three things which Negro rule gave the South:

1. Democratic government.
2. Free public schools.
3. New social legislation.

Life in South Carolina and Mississippi

Two states will illustrate conditions of government in the South before and after Negro rule. In South Carolina there was before the war a property qualification for officeholders, and, in part, for voters. The Constitution of 1868, on the other hand, was a modern democratic document starting (in marked contrast to the old constitutions) with a declaration that "We, the People," framed it, and preceded by a broad Declaration of Rights which did away with property qualifications and based representation directly upon population instead of property. It especially took up new subjects of social legislation, declaring navigable rivers free public highways, instituting homestead exemptions, establishing boards of county commissioners, providing for a new penal code of laws, establishing universal manhood suffrage "without distinction of race or color," devoting six sections to charitable and penal institutions and six to corporations, providing separate property for married women, etc. Above all, eleven sections of the Tenth Article were devoted to the establishment of a complete public-school system.

So satisfactory was the constitution thus adopted by Negro suffrage and by a convention composed of a majority of blacks that the state lived twenty-seven years under it without essential change and when the constitution was revised in 1895, the revision was practically nothing more than an amplification of the Constitution of 1868. No essential advance step of the former document was changed except the suffrage article.

In Mississippi the Constitution of 1868 was, as compared with that before the war, more democratic. It not only forbade distinctions on account of color but abolished all property qualifications for jury service, and property and educational qualifications for office; it prohibited the lending of the credit of the state for private corporations—an abuse dating back as far as 1830. It increased the powers of the governor, raised the low state salaries, and increased the number of state officials. New ideas like the public-school system and the immigration bureau were introduced and in general the activity of the state greatly and necessarily enlarged. Finally, that was the only constitution ever submitted in popular approval at the polls. This constitution remained in force twenty-two years.

In general the words of Judge Albion W. Tourgee, a "carpet-bagger," are true when he says of the Negro governments:

> They obeyed the Constitution of the United States, and annulled the bonds of states, counties, and cities which had been

issued to carry on the war of rebellion and maintain armies in the field against the Union. They instituted a public school system in a realm where public schools had been unknown. They opened the ballot box and jury box to thousands of white men who had been debarred from them by a lack of earthly possessions. They introduced home rule to the South. They abolished the whipping post, the branding iron, the stocks and other barbarous forms of punishment which had up to that time prevailed. They reduced capital felonies from about twenty to two or three. In an age of extravagance they were extravagant in the sums appropriated for public works. In all of that time no man's rights of person were invaded under the forms of law. Every Democrat's life, home, fireside and business were safe. No man obstructed any white man's way to the ballot box, interfered with his freedom of speech, or boycotted him on account of his political faith.

A thorough study of the legislation accompanying these constitutions and its changes since would of course be necessary before a full picture of the situation could be given. This has not been done, but so far as my studies have gone I have been surprised at the comparatively small amount of change in law and government which the overthrow of Negro rule brought about. . . .

The Greatest Compliment

Paint the "carpet-bag" governments and Negro rule as black as may be, the fact remains that the essence of the revolution which the overturning of the Negro governments made was to put these black men and their friends out of power. Outside the curtailing of expenses and stopping of extravagance, not only did their successors make few changes in the work which these legislatures and conventions had done, but they largely carried out their plans, followed their suggestions, and strengthened their institutions. Practically the whole new growth of the South has been accomplished under laws which black men helped to frame thirty years ago. I know of no greater compliment to Negro suffrage.

Viewpoint 3

"Every form and suggestion of social equality was resented and resisted by the whites with the energy of despair."

Reconstruction Demoralized the White South

William Archibald Dunning

William Archibald Dunning was one of the most prominent American historians of the late-nineteenth and early-twentieth centuries. His arguments that freedmen were incapable of ruling themselves and that segregation during Reconstruction was necessary shaped historical writings on the era until the 1960s, when John Hope Franklin and other revisionist historians started to argue against Dunning's claims.

In his seminal work, *Reconstruction, Political and Economic: 1865–1877*, Dunning argues that Reconstruction was a time of great demoralization among southern whites. According to Dunning, white despair and animosity toward blacks can be attributed to the chaos created by the newly established state governments, administrations run primarily by freedmen and white Republicans who had emigrated from the North (also known as carpetbaggers). Dunning asserts that the Republican administrations of Virginia, North Carolina, South Carolina, and Louisiana were beset by bribery and election fraud. He concludes that the failings of these governments showed white Americans that black suffrage and rule by carpetbaggers was the wrong way to rebuild the South.

The demoralization in the South was less political than social in its essence—that the antithesis and antipathy of race and color were crucial and ineradicable. Intelligence and political capacity were, indeed, almost exclusively in the one race; but this was not the key to the situation, for the relations of the higher class of whites with the blacks were notoriously far less hostile than those of the lower class. A map of the Ku-Klux operations which gave occasion for the enforcement acts does not touch the region of the great plantations and the black belts, where the aristocracy had their homes, but includes only the piedmont territory, where the poor whites lived. The negroes were disliked and feared almost in exact proportion to their manifestation of intelligence and capacity. What animated the whites was pride in their race as such and a dread, partly instinctive, partly rational, lest their institutions, traditions, and ideals were to be appropriated or submerged. Whether or not this feeling and spirit were abstractly preferable to those which animated the northern idealist who preached equality, the fact that such feeling and spirit were at work must be taken squarely into account by the historian.

The Reasons for Southern Animosity

The negro had no pride of race and no aspiration or ideals save to be like the whites. With civil rights and political power, not won, but almost forced upon him, he came gradually to understand and crave those more elusive privileges that constitute social equality. A more intimate association with the other race than that which business and politics involved was the end towards which the ambition of the blacks tended consciously or unconsciously to direct itself. The manifestations of this ambition were infinite in their diversity. It played a part in the demand for mixed schools, in the legislative prohibition of discrimination between the races in hotels and theatres, and even in the hideous crime against white womanhood which now assumed new meaning in the annals of outrage. But every form and suggestion of social equality was resented and resisted by the whites with the energy of despair. The dread of it justified in their eyes modes of lawlessness which were wholly subversive of civilization. [Radical Republican] Charles Sumner devoted the last years of his life to a determined effort to prohibit by Federal law any discrimination against the blacks in hotels, theatres, railways, steamboats, schools, churches, and cemeteries. His bill did not pass Congress till 1875, after his death, but his idea was taken up and enacted into law by most of the southern radical legislatures. The laws proved unenforceable and of small direct consequence, but the discussion of them furnished rich fuel to the flames of race animosity, and nerved many a hesitating white, as well as many an ambitious black, to violent deeds for the interest of his people.

The deeper springs of southern conditions were obscured to the northern masses by the cloud of partisan prejudice which hung over the subject. The radical claim that impenitent rebels were still responsible for all the troubles in the South, through their undying hatred of the negro and of the Republican party, served as a sufficient sedative for uneasiness, so long as economic prosperity in the North disposed the minds of the masses to optimism. Yet the situation in the reconstructed states in 1873, when the second administration of President [Ulysses S.] Grant got fairly under headway, was full of justification for despair.

Reconstruction Politics

Four of the states—Tennessee, Virginia, Georgia, and North Carolina—had come under conservative control, and were gradually assuming the guise of settled and orderly communities. But of these Virginia and North Carolina were confessedly bankrupt; and in all the states still under radical control the finances were in the last stages of rottenness and chaos. The amount of the state debt was in some cases undiscoverable, because no record of bond issues had been preserved. Charges of fraud, bribery, and stealing constituted the burden of political discussion in every state. Three governors had been subjected to impeachment: [William W.]Holden, of North Carolina, and [Henry C.] Warmoth, of Louisiana, were convicted and deposed; [Harrison] Reed, of Florida, was acquitted, not, apparently, so much on the ground of innocence as for the purpose of preventing the succession of a conservative. Every election, state or national, was attended by charges on both sides of fraud, intimidation, and outrage. Disputes as to the results in 1872 were followed by the occupation of three state capitals—New Orleans, Montgomery, and Little Rock—by United States troops under the general direction of Attorney-General Williams. This officer's opinions on legal and political questions became practically a decisive factor in the result of every southern state election.

South Carolina and Louisiana were in 1873 the spectacular illustrations of the working of reconstruction. The former state was thoroughly Africanized. A native white man, Franklin J. Moses, Jr., of notoriously bad character, succeeded the carpet-bagger [Robert Kingston] Scott as governor, but most of the other elected executive officers, two-thirds of the legislature, and four out of the five congressmen were negroes. The shameless caricature of government which had prevailed at Columbia since the blacks came to power was now known in its general features throughout the North. The disgust which it might have been expected to inspire was subdued, however, by the feeling that the original secessionists were meeting deserved retribution. Pathetic appeals of the small body of decent white men who were still striving to maintain their rights and their property against the flood of barbarism went unnoticed. President Grant, who found abundant ground for interfering in other states, met the prayer of a delegation from South Carolina with a *non possumus* ["we cannot"] in which the *nolumus*["we don't want to"] was unconcealed.

The situation in Louisiana was more dramatic than that in South Carolina. Henry C. Warmoth, the carpet-bagger who was elected governor in 1868, became involved during his term in a violent faction fight with adversaries in his own party headed by [Stephen B.] Packard, the United States marshal. In the election of 1872 Warmoth became a Liberal and supported the conservative state ticket against the radicals, who had the favor of President Grant. The result of the election depended chiefly on the returning board, and the legal composition of this body was in dispute. Warmoth, in an exceedingly bitter and unscrupulous conflict in the state courts, clearly outpointed his adversaries and secured a canvass of the returns by his own board, giving the presidential electors, the governorship, and the legislature to the conservatives. But Packard appealed to the United States district judge, [Edward] Durell, who, in a grossly irregular way, prohibited the conservative legislature to meet, ordered Federal troops to occupy their hall and prevent their meeting, and directed a canvass of the returns of the election by a board which he said was the legal one. Warmoth took care that this board should not get possession of the actual returns, but a canvass was nevertheless made of affidavits, census reports, and politicians' guesses, and the radical electors, governor, and legislature were declared elected.

Thus double electoral returns were sent to Washington, and two governments were organized in New Orleans. The radical legislature went through the form of impeaching and deposing Warmoth, recognized the mulatto [Benton Stewart] Pinchback as his temporary successor, and finally installed [William Pitt] Kellogg, another carpet-bagger, as the duly elected governor. The conservative legislature recognized Warmoth till the end of his term, in January, 1873, and then installed [John] McEnery, their candidate, as governor. The president, urged by his brother-in-law, Casey, collector of the port at New Orleans, and by Packard, the United States marshal, recognized Pinchback and Kellogg, and directed the troops to protect them. Later he referred the matter to Congress, where it became a subject of hot factional conflict within the Republican majority. In counting the electoral votes in February, 1873, the two houses refused to accept either return from Louisiana. The Senate committee on elections, after making a careful investigation, denounced in unmeasured terms the proceeding of Judge Durell, but failed to find a basis for definitive recognition of either of the state governments, and advised that another election be held. No measure for this purpose could be passed, and Louisiana remained in anarchy. The city of New Orleans and the white population generally recognized the McEnery government; the blacks under their carpet-bagger chiefs recognized Kellogg. In the rural districts of the state serious collisions between the races were caused by the disputes about the offices. Most disastrous was the affair at Colfax, Grant Parish, in April, 1873, where in a pitched battle several white men and more than fifty negroes were killed. The troops of the United States were admittedly all that kept the whites from sweeping Kellogg and his black supporters into oblivion. Such was the situation which, even more glaringly than the conditions in South Carolina, displayed to the people of the North the *reductio ad absurdum* of reconstruction through negro suffrage and a régime of carpet-baggers.

Viewpoint 4

"Completion of the Reconstruction era brought victory to the southern white."

Reconstruction Demoralized the Black South

Rembert W. Patrick

In the following viewpoint Rembert W. Patrick asserts that the southern whites' triumph at the end of Reconstruction led to the demoralization of the black South. According to Patrick, white southerners regained control of the South by replacing slavery with a caste system. He claims that this system demoralized southern blacks because it kept them socially, politically, and economically isolated from white Americans. Patrick argues that national support for racist views and African American leader Booker T. Washington's support of the caste system helped extend racial inequality. Patrick, who died in 1967, was the chairman of the University of Florida's history department and the author or editor of several history books, including *The Reconstruction of the Nation*, from which the following viewpoint has been excerpted.

No interpretation of American history is more inaccurate than the idea which sees the end of the Reconstruction era in the removal of federal troops from Louisiana and South Carolina. The presidential, congressional, and conservative-white phases of reconstruction have been studied and restudied by biased and impartial historians. These investigators have accepted the 1877 date as the termination of reconstruction and have labeled the subsequent decades as the era of the New South. In reality, some undeterminable day during the years from 1868 to 1877 marks the beginning of the fourth and final phase of reconstruction—that phase which ended in Southerners' winning a portion of the peace. Pinpointing the exact date is impossible, for southern-style reconstruction began in the 11 states at different times.

The central theme was state and local rule by white men. The fundamental issue in the South was neither allowing a controlled Negro vote nor disfranchising the Negro. The fourth phase of reconstruction was primarily a movement to place the Negro in an inferior position—politically, economically, and socially. It substituted a caste system for slavery. In the process of accomplishing this end, white Southerners successfully negated the Fourteenth and Fifteenth amendments. Those Negroes who broke, or were accused of breaking, state and local laws found themselves sentenced by venal judges to months and years of servitude. Blinded by racial bias, judges and courts authorized peonage, instituting a modified form of slavery for a minority of Negroes despite the Thirteen Amendment. . . .

The Popularity of Racist Writers

All over the South the means to mold public opinion belonged to those who condemned the Negro. Southern planters claimed that the freed Negro was less efficient than the slave; southern governors told reporters that the Negro was gradually becoming less productive. Newspapers reported criminal acts of Negroes but not their religious, social, and educational activities. Vilifiers possessed many voices, the defenders of the race few.

Works of racist authors found favor in North and South. Detractors of the Negroid race won temporary recognition from their books, titles of which often indicated the thesis: Charles Carroll for

Negro a Beast (1900), William P. Calhoun for *Caucasian and the Negro in the United States* (1902), William B. Smith for *Color Line: A Brief in Behalf of the Unborn* (1905), and Robert W. Shufeldt for *Negro, a Menace to American Civilization* (1907). Three of these books were published by northern firms and one by a Missouri publisher.

Thomas Dixon, however, won more than fleeting fame with a pseudohistorical trilogy of hate. Born at Shelby, North Carolina, he became a Baptist minister in 1886 and three years later accepted an appointment at a church in New York City, where he remained for ten years. A militant Southerner and racial bigot, he expressed his views in three novels: *The Leopard's Spot: A Romance of the White Man's Burden—1865–1900* (1902), *The Clansman: An Historical Romance of the Ku Klux Klan* (1905), and *The Traitor: A Story of the Fall of the Invisible Empire* (1907). Broadway audiences applauded *The Clansman* in stage version, and ten years later David W. Griffith used it to produce the first notable full-length American movie, *The Birth of a Nation*. Three generations of theatergoers eventually watched the film portray Negro bestiality and white gentility. Millions of Northerners accepted this version as the correct interpretation of the Reconstruction period.

At home and abroad the Negro was dominated by the white race. European imperialism awoke and surpassed its former vigor. Africa was partitioned, parts of Asia were grabbed, and almost every other underdeveloped area of the world became the possession or economic dependency of some country. The "white man's burden" thesis justified territorial acquisitions and economic gains, and extended white supremacy.

The Spanish-American War drew the United States reluctantly into the new imperialism. In contrast to former territorial additions, the nation acquired noncontiguous, overseas lands, densely populated by alien races. In a series of decisions known as the "Insular Cases," the Supreme Court decreed that guarantees of the Constitution did not follow the American flag. At the same time the federal government was spending millions of dollars to subdue the Philippine insurrectionists. Then [South Carolina senator] Ben Tillman accused [Massachusetts senator] Henry Cabot Lodge, almost the sole senator still advocating some protection for southern Negroes, of shedding crocodile tears for "black babies" of the South while voting funds to kill the "brown babies" of the Philippine Islands.

The United States accepted the southern ideas of racial superiority. After the passage of almost a century, white Southerners again enjoyed the pleasant midstream waters of Caucasian history.

Booker T. Washington's Views

The caste system of the United States was accepted by a Negro leader, Booker T. Washington. His mother was a mulatto slave and his father a white man. After emancipation, Washington labored in salt and coal mines of West Virginia until he entered and worked his way through Hampton Institute. After teaching and additional study, he was selected in 1881 to organize a school for Negroes in Alabama. At Tuskegee Institute he made famous an institution for Negro industrial training. Ability as a speaker and a pleasing personality gave him access to white audiences and association with males and females of the white society. Personal success perhaps convinced Washington that Southerners would ignore skin color and recognize individual accomplishments.

A speech in 1895 to a racially mixed audience in the Atlanta Cotton States and International Exposition won him national acclaim. "I was born in the South," he said, "and I understand thoroughly the prejudices, the customs, the traditions of the South [and love the region]." He advocated many policies: agitation of Negroes for social equality was folly; northern intervention in southern affairs was misdirected humanitarianism; reforms in the Southland should come from white Southerners; and Negroes were more interested in industrial education and economic opportunity than in casting ballots or serving in state legislatures. Rewards would come to Negroes, he said, if they proved themselves worthy by "severe and constant struggle" to deserve recognition.

Washington urged members of his race to forge ahead in agriculture, mechanics, commerce, domestic service, and the professions. He warned them not to forget in the great leap from slavery to freedom that manual labor was still their main source of livelihood: "No race can prosper till it learns that there is as much dignity in tilling a field as in writing a poem. It is at the bottom of life we must begin, and not at the top." He asked white people not to rely on aliens with their strange language and habits, but on the 8 million Negroes, a people who had proven their loyalty in peace and war.

Washington's willingness to yield political and civil rights and his promotion of a type of education most likely to keep the Negro economically and socially subordinate to the white endeared him to southern leaders. By overlooking mistreatment, by emphasizing the best past performances of whites and relying on them to treat the Negro fairly, and by advising his people to labor, elevate themselves, and be law-abiding, he won the hearts of

Greater Changes in the North

[Reconstruction] had brought changes, to be sure, but most of them had taken place in the North. The section that had expressed deep feelings about slavery and human degradation and had gone to war to preserve the Union had itself been transformed. It was now an industrial colossus with new values, new leadership, and new aspirations. No longer was it interested in activities that might distract or disturb its phenomenal growth and expansion. The South, having changed much less, was more than ever attached to the values and outlook that had shaped its history. Even its once-belligerent adversary was now conciliatory. On the points most important to the white South the North was willing to yield; and on the points most important to the North the white South was willing to yield. In a sense, then, both sides were pleased with the outcome of reconstruction. In another sense, however, both sides suffered an ignoble defeat. The Union had been preserved and human slavery had been abolished; but these were achievements of the war. In the postwar years the Union had not made the achievements of the war a foundation for the healthy advancement of the political, social, and economic life of the United States.

John Hope Franklin, *Reconstruction: After the Civil War*. Chicago: University of Chicago Press, 1961.

southern whites. His ideas meshed well with Social Darwinism; Negroes would demonstrate their fitness for leadership or become mudsill laborers. But whites ignored the ultimate goal of his program—eventual integration of Negroes into American society.

After more than half a century it is difficult to evaluate Washington. He won fame and power unparalleled in the history of his race. Federal authorities and heads of philanthropic agencies turned to him for approval of Negro applicants for jobs and welfare projects. At times so dictatorial that few Negro individuals or newspapers dared to criticize him, his word could dash hopes and wreck projects; but his recommendations secured economic opportunity for thousands and won millions of dollars for educational and other projects of his people. He appeared at a critical time—the Negro was being disfranchised, hounded, shorn of civil rights, almost abandoned by Northerners, and hated by southern extremists. By accepting caste, perhaps the Negro lost nothing he had not already lost or was in the process of losing. Washington's "Atlanta Compromise" eased racial tension and gave the Negro time to build a base for a fight for his rights as an American.

But Washington riveted the iron mask of caste on his people. He neither originated the caste system nor conceived of it as a permanent arrangement. His greatest failure was his optimistic appraisal of his white countrymen. Most southern and many northern whites had no intention of granting first-class citizenship to any Negro, however successful he was in demonstrating his right to equal status. For these people the color of one's skin classified him.

The Triumph of the Caste System

For almost half a century following the Civil War, equality under law was the subject of debate and experiment. Former secessionists and Confederates relegated freedmen to a status similar to that occupied by the free Negro in the ante-bellum South. Northerners gave the Negro a taste of political and civil equality, but did little to aid him economically. Despite their confusing verbiage, the principal objections of conservative white Southerners to Congressional Reconstruction were enfranchisement of the Negro and federal protection of the freedman. No knowledgeable southern white believed that the "bottom rail had been placed on top"; at the high-water mark of Congressional Reconstruction, Negroes remained economically, politically, and socially subordinate to the white man. Absolute white supremacy motivated the southern drive for a racial settlement. By the early twentieth century, white Southerners won complete victory and the Negro was relegated to a status more rigorous in many respects than that of the slave or black codes.

The caste system extended Negro servitude into the twentieth century. Always a land of freedom and opportunity for white immigrants, even indentured servants and poverty-stricken peasants, America offered these wonderful gifts to comparatively few Negroes. Whatever their ambition or ability, they were held in check by slavery, restrictive custom and law, and the caste system. In February 1900, George H. White, the last Negro congressman of the Reconstruction era, replied to southern demagogues: "It is easy for these gentlemen to taunt us with our inferiority. It is rather hard to be accused of shiftlessness and idleness when the accuser closes the avenue of labor and industrial pursuits to us. It is hardly fair to accuse us of ignorance when it was a crime under the former order of things to learn enough about letters to even read the Word of God."

Completion of the Reconstruction era brought victory to the southern white, a victory which made the United States Constitution color-conscious. Southern-born Justice [John Marshall] Harlan's idea of a "color-blind" Constitution remained a goal for the future.

 **Appendix**

The Reconstruction Amendments to the U.S. Constitution

Amendment XIII

Section 1. Neither slavery nor involuntary servitude, except as a punishment for crime whereof the party shall have been duly convicted, shall exist within the United States, or any place subject to their jurisdiction.

Section 2. Congress shall have power to enforce this article by appropriate legislation.

Amendment XIV

Section 1. All persons born or naturalized in the United States, and subject to the jurisdiction thereof, are citizens of the United States and of the State wherein they reside. No State shall make or enforce any law which shall abridge the privileges or immunities of citizens of the United States; nor shall any State deprive any person of life, liberty, or property, without due process of law; nor deny to any person within its jurisdiction the equal protection of the laws.

Section 2. Representatives shall be apportioned among the several States according to their respective numbers, counting the whole number of persons in each State, excluding Indians not taxed. But when the right to vote at any election for the choice of electors for President and Vice President of the United States, representatives in Congress, the executive and judicial officers of a State, or the members of the legislature thereof, is denied to any of the male inhabitants of such State, being twenty-one years of age, and citizens of the United States, or in any way abridged, except for participating in rebellion, or other crime, the basis of representation therein shall be reduced in the proportion which the number of such male citizens shall bear to the whole number of male citizens twenty-one years of age in such State.

Section 3. No person shall be senator or representative in Congress, or elector of President and Vice President, or hold any office, civil or military, under the United States, or under any State, who having previously taken an oath, as a member of Congress, or as an officer of the United States, or as a member of any State legislature, or as an executive or judicial officer of any State, to support the Constitution of the United States, shall have engaged in insurrection or rebellion against the same, or given aid or comfort to the enemies thereof. But Congress may by a vote of two thirds of each House, remove such disability.

Section 4. The validity of the public debt of the United States, authorized by law, including debts incurred for payment of pensions and bounties for services in suppressing insurrection or rebellion, shall not be questioned. But neither the United States nor any State shall assume or pay any debt or obligation incurred in aid of insurrection or rebellion against the United States, or any claim for the loss or emancipation of any slave; but all such debts, obligations, and claims shall be held illegal and void.

Section 5. The Congress shall have the power to enforce, by appropriate legislation, the provisions of this article.

Amendment XV

Section 1. The right of the citizens of the United States to vote shall not be denied or abridged by the United States or by any State on account of race, color, or previous condition of servitude.

Section 2. The Congress shall have power to enforce this article by appropriate legislation.

For Further Discussion

Chapter One

1. Abraham Lincoln and Henry Winter Davis disagree on which branch of the government should have authority over Reconstruction. If you had to engineer a Reconstruction strategy based on a compromise between the two plans, what details would you include in such a proposal?
2. Andrew Johnson asserts that the United States and the Constitution are inextricably linked and that destroying one will cause the other to also perish. Do you agree with his opinion? Why or why not?
3. Gabor S. Boritt and Avery Craven examine President Lincoln's reconstruction plan in their viewpoints. After reading their selections, do you think that Lincoln would have successfully rebuilt the United States had he not been assassinated? Why or why not?

Chapter Two

1. In his viewpoint, Andrew J. Rogers argues that the Fourteenth Amendment should not be approved because it will violate states' rights, such as their prerogative to pass discriminatory laws. Do you think that states should be able to pass any legislation they want or should the federal government be able to dictate what state laws are enacted? Explain your answer, drawing from this and any other relevant viewpoints.
2. Alexander White and William Manning Lowe debate the effect of carpetbaggers on southern life and politics. How do you think Reconstruction would have been different had Radical Republicans not moved to the South from the North? Do you believe that southern Republicans would have been able to build state governments without the support of northern transplants? Explain your answers.
3. After reading the viewpoints by Chester G. Hearn and Eric Foner, which party do you believe is more to blame for the fail-

ure of Andrew Johnson's reconstruction plans: the president or his Radical Republican opponents? Explain your answer.

Chapter Three

1. Frederick Douglass asserts that blacks should have the right to vote because they helped the North win the Civil War. Do you agree with his argument? Explain your answer.
2. The Freedmen's Bureau provided the majority of educational funding for freed slaves. Do you think that George Fitzhugh's criticisms of black education are more valid because he is a former agent of the bureau? Why or why not?
3. After reading the viewpoints by Loren Schweninger and Chester J. Wynne, how would you characterize life for African Americans in the first two decades after the Civil War? Explain your answer.

Chapter Four

1. After reading the viewpoints in this chapter do you believe that Reconstruction changed America for the better? Why or why not?
2. In their viewpoints, William Archibald Dunning and Rembert W. Patrick debate the effects of Reconstruction on white and black southerners. Dunning wrote his perspective in 1907, thirty years after the end of Reconstruction, and lived during that era. Patrick wrote in the 1960s, a hundred years after Reconstruction began. Do you believe that Dunning's understanding of Reconstruction is more nuanced because he was alive during that time, or do you think that Patrick offers a more accurate perspective because the ensuing decades helped eliminate the potential for personal bias? Explain your answers.

 **Chronology**

January 1, 1863
President Abraham Lincoln signs the Emancipation Proclamation.

December 8, 1863
Lincoln announces his Proclamation of Amnesty, which delineates his 10 Percent Plan for reconstruction.

July 2, 1864
Congress passes the Wade-Davis Bill, which is designed to give Congress control over reconstruction. Lincoln pocket-vetoes the bill two days later.

November 8, 1864
President Lincoln is reelected to a second term.

January 16, 1865
General William T. Sherman issues Special Field Order Number 15, which sets aside portions of southern land for the exclusive settlement of the freed slaves.

January 31, 1865
Congress approves the Thirteenth Amendment by a vote of 119-56.

March 3, 1865
The Bureau for Refugees, Freedmen, and Abandoned Lands, known as the Freedmen's Bureau, is established by an act of Congress.

April 9, 1865
Confederate general Robert E. Lee surrenders to Union general Ulysses S. Grant at Appomattox Courthouse.

April 11, 1865
President Lincoln delivers his last public address, in which he endorses limited black suffrage.

April 14, 1865

Lincoln is shot by John Wilkes Booth: He dies the next day. Three hours after Lincoln's death, Vice President Andrew Johnson takes the presidential oath of office.

May 29, 1865

President Johnson announces his reconstruction policy, which grants pardons to former Rebels who pledge loyalty to the Union.

July 1865

General Oliver Howard, commissioner of the Freedmen's Bureau, issues Circular 13 instructing bureau agents to set aside forty-acre tracts of land for the freedmen.

September 1865

Johnson instructs Howard to rescind Circular 13. In October, Howard announces to black settlers that their land will be returned to the original white owners.

November 24, 1865

Mississippi becomes the first state to enact a Black Code. Most of the other southern states shortly follow suit.

December 18, 1865

The Thirteenth Amendment is ratified.

April 9, 1866

Overriding a presidential veto, Congress passes the Civil Rights Act of 1866.

May 1–3, 1866

A major race riot erupts in Memphis, Tennessee; forty-six blacks and two white Unionists are killed.

June 13, 1866

Congress approves the Fourteenth Amendment.

July 24, 1866

Congress readmits Tennessee to the Union.

July 30, 1866
A race riot breaks out in New Orleans. Thirty-four blacks and three white Radicals are among the forty casualties.

November 1866
Republicans sweep the congressional elections, providing them with the majority needed to consistently override presidential vetoes.

March 2, 1867
Congress enacts two bills over Johnson's veto: the First Reconstruction Act, which divides the former Confederacy into five military districts, and the Tenure of Office Act, which prohibits the president from dismissing a cabinet officer without the Senate's consent.

March 23, 1867
The Second Reconstruction Act is passed by Congress over a presidential veto.

July 19, 1867
Congress passes the Third Reconstruction Act over a presidential veto.

August 12, 1867
President Johnson suspends War Secretary Edwin Stanton and asks the Senate to agree to his dismissal under the terms of the Tenure of Office Act.

November 5, 1867
In Montgomery, Alabama, the first reconstruction state constitutional convention begins. During the following months, all of the former Confederate states hold conventions.

January 13, 1868
The Senate declines to remove Stanton from his cabinet office.

February 21, 1868
Johnson dismisses Stanton, who refuses to leave and barricades himself in his office.

February 24, 1868
The House of Representatives votes 126-47 to impeach President Johnson.

March 11, 1868
Congress passes the Fourth Reconstruction Act.

March 13, 1868
Johnson's impeachment trial begins.

May 28, 1868
The Senate acquits President Johnson of high crimes and misdemeanors.

June 22–25, 1868
Congress readmits Alabama, Arkansas, North Carolina, South Carolina, Louisiana, Florida, and Georgia to the Union.

July 21, 1868
The Fourteenth Amendment is ratified.

September 1868
After Georgia's state government removes its black members, Congress returns Georgia to military rule.

November 3, 1868
General Ulysses S. Grant is elected president.

February 26, 1869
Congress approves the Fifteenth Amendment.

January 20, 1870
Hiram R. Revels of Mississippi is elected as the first black U.S. senator.

January 26, 1870
Congress readmits Virginia to the Union.

February 23, 1870
Mississippi is readmitted to the Union.

March 30, 1870
The Fifteenth Amendment is ratified. In the following months, several southern states pass poll-tax laws that are designed to

reduce the effectiveness of the Fifteenth Amendment by restricting black voters. Texas is readmitted to the Union.

May 31, 1870
Congress passes the First Enforcement Act in an effort to deal with increasing violence and civil rights violations in the South.

July 15, 1870
Congress readmits Georgia to the Union for the second time.

October 25, 1870
In Eutaw, Alabama, whites fire into a Republican campaign rally, killing four blacks and wounding fifty.

February 28, 1871
Congress passes the Second Enforcement Act.

March 4, 1871
The first black representatives to the U.S. Congress take their seats. They are Joseph H. Rainey, Robert DeLarge, Robert Brown Elliot, Benjamin S. Turner, and Josiah T. Walls.

March 6–7, 1871
In Meridian, Mississippi, a white Republican judge and more than thirty blacks are killed during a race riot.

April 20, 1871
Congress passes the Third Enforcement Act, also called the Ku Klux Klan Act.

October 17, 1871
President Grant sends federal troops to South Carolina to put down the Ku Klux Klan.

May 22, 1872
Congress passes the Amnesty Act, which removes political disabilities from all but approximately five hundred of the most prominent former Confederates.

June 10, 1872
The Freedmen's Bureau Act is allowed to expire, and the bureau is dissolved.

November 5, 1872
In a landslide victory, President Grant is elected to a second term.

December 9, 1872
P.B.S. Pinchback of Louisiana becomes the first black governor in America when Louisiana's sitting governor is suspended due to impeachment proceedings.

April 13, 1873
On Easter Sunday, more than sixty blacks are killed by armed whites in Colfax, Louisiana.

April 14, 1873
In the Slaughterhouse Cases, the U.S. Supreme Court rules that the Fourteenth Amendment protects only those rights that derive from federal—not state—citizenship.

September 18, 1873
The failure of a major banking firm triggers the Panic of 1873, an economic depression that persists for five years.

November 4, 1874
Democrats sweep the congressional elections and gain a majority in the House of Representatives.

December 7, 1874
On December 7 and the following days, bands of armed whites kill an estimated three hundred blacks in Vicksburg, Mississippi.

January 5, 1875
President Grant dispatches federal troops to Vicksburg, Mississippi.

February 3, 1875
Blanche K. Bruce is elected to the U.S. Senate, bringing black representation in Congress to its peak of eight.

March 1, 1875
Congress passes the Civil Rights Act of 1875, which outlaws segregation.

March 1875
Congress fails to pass a Fourth Enforcement Bill before adjourning.

September 4–6, 1875
Thirty blacks and three whites are killed in a race riot in Clinton, Mississippi.

March 27, 1876
In *U.S. v. Cruikshank*, the U.S. Supreme Court overturns convictions under the Enforcement Acts of 1870, ruling that the federal government can only prohibit civil rights violations by the states, not by private individuals.

July 8, 1876
A race riot in Hamburg, South Carolina, results in the deaths of seven blacks.

September 20, 1876
A race riot erupts in Ellenton, South Carolina; several whites and approximately one hundred blacks are killed.

October 16, 1876
Six whites and one black die in a race riot in Cainhoy, South Carolina.

October 26, 1876
Grant sends federal troops to intervene in South Carolina.

November 7, 1876
The presidential election results in a dispute over who won.

February 26, 1877
The Compromise of 1877 secures Republican Rutherford B. Hayes's claim to the presidency in exchange for the return of home rule to the South.

April 24, 1877
Hayes withdraws the last federal troops from the South.

February 1879
The Exodus Movement begins.

October 15, 1883

The Supreme Court declares the Civil Rights Act of 1875 unconstitutional, opening the way for the passage of numerous "Jim Crow" laws.

February 8, 1894

Congress repeals the Second Enforcement Act, thereby giving the states direct control over elections and enabling the southern states to virtually disfranchise blacks without federal interference.

May 18, 1896

In *Plessy v. Ferguson,* the Supreme Court upholds the principle of "separate but equal" racial segregation.

 **For Further Research**

Historical Studies

Eric Anderson and Alfred A. Moss Jr., eds., *The Facts of Reconstruction: Essays in Honor of John Hope Franklin*. Baton Rouge: Louisiana State University Press, 1991.

Michael Les Benedict, *The Impeachment and Trial of Andrew Johnson*. New York: Norton, 1973.

Lerone Bennett, *Black Power, U.S.A.: The Human Side of Reconstruction*. Chicago: Johnson, 1967.

Francis L. Broderick, *Reconstruction and the American Negro, 1865–1900*. London: Macmillan, 1969.

LaWanda Cox and John H. Cox, *Politics, Principle, and Prejudice, 1865–1866: Dilemma of Reconstruction America*. Glencoe, IL: Free Press, 1963.

Avery Craven, *Reconstruction: The Ending of the Civil War*. New York: Holt, Rinehart and Winston, 1969.

Robert Cruden, *The Negro in Reconstruction*. Englewood Cliffs, NJ: Prentice-Hall, 1969.

Richard N. Current, *Those Terrible Carpetbaggers*. New York: Oxford University Press, 1988.

W.E.B. Du Bois, *Black Reconstruction in America: 1860–1880*. New York: Russell & Russell, 1935.

William Dunning, *Essays on the Civil War and Reconstruction*. New York: Harper & Row, 1965.

———, *Reconstruction, Political and Economic, 1865– 1877*. New York: Harper, 1907.

Eric Foner, *Reconstruction: America's Unfinished Revolution, 1863–1877*. New York: Harper & Row, 1988.

John Hope Franklin, *Reconstruction: After the Civil War*. Chicago: University of Chicago Press, 1961.

Chester G. Hearn, *The Impeachment of Andrew Johnson*. Jefferson, NC: McFarland, 2000.

Robert H. Jones, *Disrupted Decades: The Civil War and Reconstruction Years*. New York: Charles Scribner's Sons, 1973.

Charles H. McCarthy, *Lincoln's Plan of Reconstruction*. New York: AMS Press, 1966.

Eric McKitrick, *Andrew Johnson and Reconstruction*. Chicago: University of Chicago Press, 1960.

James M. McPherson, *Ordeal by Fire: The Civil War and Reconstruction*. New York: Knopf, 1982.

James Mohr, ed., *Radical Republicans in the North: State Politics During Reconstruction*. Baltimore: Johns Hopkins University Press, 1976.

Howard P. Nash Jr., *Andrew Johnson: Congress and Reconstruction*. Cranbury, NJ: Associated University Presses, 1972.

Rembert W. Patrick, *The Reconstruction of the Nation*. London: Oxford University Press, 1967.

Michael Perman, *Reunion Without Compromise: The South and Reconstruction, 1865–1868*. New York: Cambridge University Press, 1973.

Heather Cox Richardson, *The Death of Reconstruction: Race, Labor, and Politics in the Post–Civil War North, 1865–1901*. Cambridge, MA: Harvard University Press, 2001.

Edwin C. Rozwenc, *Reconstruction in the South*. Lexington, MA: D.C. Heath, 1972.

Kenneth Stampp, *The Era of Reconstruction, 1865–1877*. New York: Knopf, 1965.

Richard Taylor, *Destruction and Reconstruction*. New York: Da-Capo Press, 1995.

Hans Trefousse, *The Radical Republicans: Lincoln's Vanguard for Social Justice.* New York: Knopf, 1969.

———, *Reconstruction: America's First Effort at Racial Democracy.* New York: Van Nostrand Reinhold, 1971.

Allen W. Trelease, *White Terror: The Ku Klux Klan Conspiracy and Southern Reconstruction.* New York: Harper & Row, 1971.

William P. Vaughan, *Schools for All: The Blacks and Public Education in the South, 1865–1877.* Lexington: University Press of Kentucky, 1974.

Primary Sources and Document Collections

Sidney Andrews, *The South Since the War.* Boston: Ticknor and Fields, 1866.

John W. Blassingame and John R. McKivigan, eds., *The Frederick Douglass Papers, Series One: Speeches, Debates, and Interviews: Volume 4, 1864–80.* New Haven, CT: Yale University Press, 1991.

LaWanda Cox and John H. Cox, eds., *Reconstruction, the Negro, and the New South.* Columbia: University of South Carolina Press, 1973.

Richard N. Current, ed., *Reconstruction, 1865–1877.* Englewood Cliffs, NJ: Prentice-Hall, 1965.

Philip Foner, ed., *The Life and Writings of Frederick Douglass.* New York: International Publishers, 1950.

Harold Hyman, ed., *The Radical Republicans and Reconstruction, 1861–1870.* Indianapolis: Bobbs-Merrill, 1967.

Robert W. Johannsen, ed., *Reconstruction, 1865–1877.* New York: Free Press, 1970.

Glenn M. Linden, *Voices from the Reconstruction Years, 1865–1877.* Fort Worth, TX: Harcourt Brace College Publishers, 1999.

Annjennette Sophie McFarlin, *Black Congressional Reconstruction*

Orators and Their Orations, 1869–1879. Metuchen, NJ: Scarecrow Press, 1976.

Michael Perman, ed., *Major Problems in the Civil War and Reconstruction: Documents and Essays.* Lexington, MA: D.C. Heath, 1991.

James S. Pike, *The Prostrate State: South Carolina Under Negro Government.* New York: D. Appleton, 1874.

Carl Schurz, *Report on the Condition of the South.* New York: Arno Press, 1969.

Dorothy Sterling, ed., *The Trouble They Seen: Black People Tell the Story of Reconstruction.* Garden City, NY: Doubleday, 1976.

Harvey Wish, ed., *Reconstruction in the South, 1865–1877.* New York: Farrar, Straus & Giroux, 1965.

Carter G. Woodson, ed., *Negro Orators and Their Orations.* New York: Russell & Russell, 1969.

Websites

The Andrew Johnson Impeachment Trial, http://www.law.umkc.edu/faculty/projects/ftrials/impeach/impeachmt.htm. Compiled by a professor at the University of Missouri at Kansas City School of Law, this site provides extensive information on the Johnson impeachment trial, including a trial record, opinions by various senators, and links to articles from 1860s' issues of *Harper's Weekly.*

Reconstruction and Rights, http://memory.loc.gov/ammem/ndlpedu/features/timeline/civilwar/recontwo/recontwo.html. The Library of Congress runs this website. It features a collection of primary documents, including speeches and interviews, and focuses on voting rights in the South.

Index